GERMAN ARTILLERY
In World War II
1939-1945

Joachim Engelmann

The aiming gunner is responsible for reliable precision and quick reaction of fire. He is also the gun leader, as seen here in Russia, February 1944.

GERMAN ARTILLERY In World War II 1939-1945

Joachim Engelmann

Schiffer Military/Aviation History
Atglen, PA

Dust jacket artwork by Steve Ferguson, Colorado Springs, CO
Additional research by Russell Mueller

STING OF THE HUMMEL

By late 1942, the scope and ferocity of the European war brought demand for heavier caliber artillery pieces to support the embattled Wehrmacht troops. One of the most successful upgrade weapons available by late 1943 was the Panzerfeldhaubitze Sd.Kfz.165, more commonly known by its nickname, the "Hummel" (bumblebee).

The Hummel was a modified Panzer IV manned by a crew of five or six who serviced the 150mm howitzer which fired a 96 pound projectile. Although it first re-equipped units of the the Waffen-SS on the eastern front, the 23-ton open-turret Sd.Kfz.165 was never intended to be an attack vehicle. It soon became the mainstay of premier panzer divisions in Russia and the Mediterranean theatres.

The veteran artillery crews of them elite Hermann Göring Division in Italy proved the Hummel to be a devastating stand-off weapon against the pursuing American 5th Army. Many a Yank would fall in the Italian campaign, particularly when the contested mountain passes and villages were ze-roed-in by a battalion of Hummels, eight miles from the target. Because the Hummels were in direct fire units and highly mobile, they were rarely captured at a battle site. Long-range artillery exchanges and Allied aircraft were the scourge of the Hummel crews.

Our scene depicts a pair of "russet on yellow" camouflaged Hummels of the Hermann Göring Division laying in a barrage on a mountian road, somewhere in the terraced hills near Cassino. The gun commander has stepped up on the ammo crate in the turret to better survey the results of their work. After sweating out a 150mm night barrage south of Rome, American war correspondent and humorist Bill Maudlin aptly questioned, "Why do we always catch 'em, just to make 'em run again?"

Translated from the German by Edward Force.

This book was originally published under the title,
Das Buch der Artillerie,
by Podzun-Pallas Verlag.

Printed in the United States of America.
ISBN: 0-88740-762-5

We are interested in hearing from authors with book ideas on related topics.

Published by Schiffer Publishing Ltd.
77 Lower Valley Road
Atglen, PA 19310
Please write for a free catalog.
This book may be purchased from the publisher.
Please include $2.95 postage.
Try your bookstore first.

Contents

Foreword

It is not generally known that German artillery never before attained such size, variety and extent as those from 1939 to 1945. From North Cape to Tobruk, the Bay of Biscay to Lapland, Den Helder to the Caucasus, its units fought during those six years, with the following overall strength:

1023 light and ca. 340 heavy horse-drawn units,
58 light and 48 heavy field howitzer units (motorized),
38 mixed field howitzer units (self-propelled mounts),
100 assault gun/assault artillery brigades, 15 lone batteries,
96 observation units, 38 armored observation batteries,
1 light-measuring battery, 16 other observation batteries,
66 army anti-aircraft units,
1177 army coastal batteries,
45 railroad batteries,
ca. 400 light and heavy army artillery units (motorized), without fortress artillery, regimental staffs and lone batteries,
20 survey and map units, 1 survey battery, 5 map-printing units, 1 printing platoon,
30 mountain artillery units,
13 army antitank artillery units,
8 light gun units,
49 launcher regiments, 25 independent launcher units, long-range A 4 (V 2) rocket units.

Army anti-aircraft gun and launcher troops even became individual troop types during the war. In 1939-1940 the strength of the artillery was 483,378 men – 12.8% of the wartime army; on October 1, 1943, with 655,000 men, it was 22.6% of the army. Its portion of the entire wartime army, including the Waffen-SS, was 6.1%. Three-fourths of its units were permanently in the east. It suffered its greatest losses at Stalingrad in 1942-1943 and in the collapse of the Army Group Center in the summer of 1944. Twenty-three high commanders led the artillery of the armies, 123 commanded that of the corps. After the disbanding of the 18th Artillery Division, it acquired 27 army artillery brigades and "Peoples' Artillery Corps" for the army artillery alone. In addition to the 39 German gun types, the artillery used more than forty captured types of guns from ten different European countries. All of this was surely unique.

At this time, along with the tumultuous expansion and large-scale technical development, a great breakthrough in weapon design from the previous artillery of Wallenstein's days took place, extending to long-range rockets, as had never before happened in so short a time. This surely embodied the danger of fragmentation of powers, raw materials, funds and production.

From the spring of 1943 on, as the constantly overburdened infantry and the very embattled tank units began to lose their fighting strength, the maneuverability and firepower of the artillery grew more and more important, as the backbone of resistance and defense, all the more so as the Luftwaffe had long since lost its advantage. For that reason, it is of value for those who experienced the war, as well as those who did not, to get a good look at all its tasks, actions and everyday existence. This compilation does not want to accomplish more than that; it is not meant to be either complete or a historical evaluation or a book of military science. Reliable handiwork, surprising massive effect from under cover, and personal inconspicuousness were always characteristics of the artilleryman.

Modestia fundamentum virtutis!
Joachim Engelmann

Light Field Cannon 18 (Caliber 7.5 cm, range 9.4 km) of the "mounted unit" of a cavalry brigade moves out during the 1939 Polish campaign – the ideal conception of German artillery in peacetime! More than one quarter of all divisions were horsedrawn as infantry divisions.

Horsedrawn

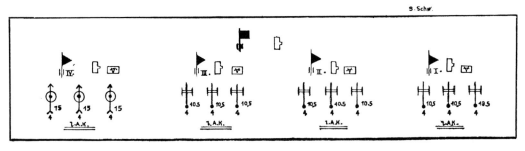

The regiment had three light units with 36 leFH 18 howitzers and one heavy unit with 12 sFH 18, moved by 2700 of the entire division's 6000 horses. The modern field howitzers, weighing between two and six tons, were much too heavy to be moved throughout Europe and through sand, snow and bottomless mud.

Horses requisitioned from farmers during the 1939 mobilization are examined by veterinarians, troop officers and paymasters, here of the I./AR 97 in Stockerau. Training in six-horse hitches came afterward.

Riding practice by drivers on Oct. 12, 1940, with courage and capability drills. Artillerymen often regarded themselves as frustrated cavalrymen.

Harness smiths are necessary personnel.

Parade formation of the III./AR 96, 44th Infantry Division.

Horse inspection, 6./AR 260, May 1941, before moving out toward the east.

The unit's veterinarian carefully examines a horse's wound in France, June 1944.

Horses and riders enjoy a rare chance to relax in the water – AR 5 in France, 1940.

Gunnery drill by cannoneers includes replacing the barrel of the sFH 18 howitzer – 10./AR 260, France, December 1940.

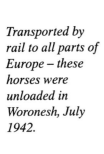

Transported by rail to all parts of Europe – these horses were unloaded in Woronesh, July 1942.

AR 5 crossing the Seine in 1940.

Endless marches require regular pauses – here AR 5 is seen at rest in September 1941.

France has capitulated, and AR 5 gathers its batteries. In a few months the regiment will head eastward.

June 22, 1941, the advance on Russia begins on a broad front. Above: III./AR 252 north of Brest. Center: II./AR 5 north of Grodno. Below: AR 178 beside the Bug.

There is scarcely enough water in the heat of summer on the Russian plains.

As night falls, AR 96, 44th Infantry Division, changes positions as villages burn in the background; the location is not known.

The artillery pushes its way ahead through dust and the smoke of burning Russian tanks.

Batteries of AR 96 set out at dawn near Nesolon in 1941.

Above: Light field howitzers (lFH 18) on the march in August 1941. Center: lFH 16 howitzers take up positions at Kursk in 1943.

Below: 7.62 cm Field Gun 296 (r), L/51, weight 1.6 tons, range 13.6 km, captured and used by infantry divisions of the 21st Wave in 1943, drawn by weak teams.

It may take ten horses to pull the leFH 18 across the fields.

Drawing water for man and beast becomes a work of art when the water freezes over the outside of the well. Below: A ten-horse hitch pulls the sFH barrel wagon of the 1./AR 97 uphill in Poland in 1939.

A gun-mount wagon of the IV./AR 260 with a double hitch, seen near Pritcheva on November 2, 1941.

The leFH 16 has been brought into position and dismounted. The limber is moved aside while the cannoneers prepare the gun for firing.

K 1 sets the ordered traverse position, while K 2 sets the elevation.

The Traverse Unteroffizier II aims the battery of six guns and give the K 2 the settings for every gun during the summer of 1943 in northern Russia.

The gun leader helps the gunner correct the aim of the gun. Below: Chief 4./AR 260 and his officers at the radio position of the firing position on the Aisne on June 9, 1940.

The telephone in the firing position provides communication with the B position and the unit.

The telephone troop leader calls out the B position's order to fire to the battery officer.

The gun leader raises his hand: "Fire!" Cannoneer 2 pulls the cord.

The battery officer, with microphone and shot tables, an experienced professional soldier, holds the gun crew together. He is responsible for the firing position, as here in Lapland in 1944.

A firing position of AR 96 on the western edge of Prishib in the winter of 1941-1942, defending against strong attacks near Balakleya.

A loader seen during a firefight on the invasion front in 1944.

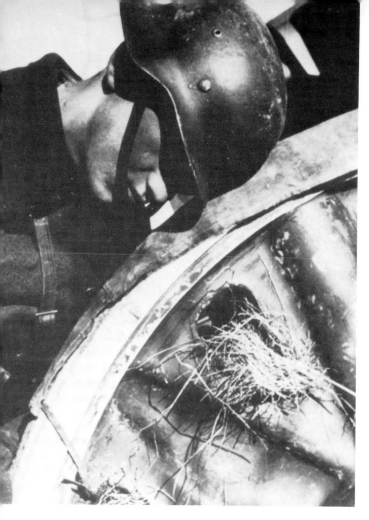

During a pause in firing, the exhausted K 2 leans on the wheel of his gun, camouflaged to avoid being spotted from the air.

The firing position of a leFH 16, with net camouflaged, near Woronesh in July 1942.

Meticulous work has splendidly camouflaged this leFH 18 at Orel in January 1942.

The cannoneers live with and beside their guns day and night. Before a planned change of positions – the ground spurs are already folded up – they quickly have a bite to eat.

Open firing positions of sFH guns of the IV./AR 205 on the upper Rhine in 1939, generally 250 meters apart.

A weapons master examines a heavy field howitzer of the IV./AR 215 on a cold January day east of Shudovo.

Cleaning a gun of the I./AR 97 after the 1939 campaign, before being transferred to the west.

Well-camouflaged firing positions of the 12./AR 263 in the Nara area near Moscow in December 1941. The fires under the mounts keep them ready for action.

The heavy field howitzer made two horse-drawn loads. The sFH barrel wagon is being towed by the mount wagon and will position the barrel over the mount when the latter is unloaded. Seen on the West Wall in the Eifel mountains, April 15, 1940.

The unloaded mount wagon stands at the left, while the men pull the barrel wagon into position. Placing the barrel in position is back-breaking work. The limber of the barrel wagon is at right.

Networks of
telephones are
needed for fire
control. Above:
the 5th Jäger
Division south of
Ilmen Lake in
1942. Below: The
252nd I.D. south
of Istra on
December 4,
1941, under
severe pressure.

The laborious erection of an important line in the frozen north, not far from Prishib, by the 1./ AR 96.

An unloading beam used as a radio antenna beside a rein-forced tent in Lapland, spring 1943, with sleds stacked at the rear.

Phone lines, destroyed often enough, were combined with radio links. Most observers worked with radio. This is the radio position of a battery near Kursk in 1943.

Radiomen of an advanced observation post of the I./AR 96 with their 30-kilogram portable radios, June 1940.

Snow and frost caused much trouble for the batteries and moisture collectors of the radio sets. Only capable radiomen could play tricks that would keep them going.

A look through a shear telescope at the enemy's position and the hotly contested ruins at Vyshnoye.

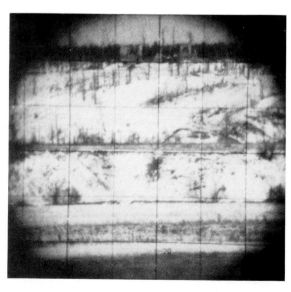

The artillery is commanded from the front. From the gable of a house, a battery chief or observation officer observes the enemy's terrain in February 1944.

Artillery observers in a trench, amid snow and ice, in Lapland, 1943-1944.

An observer hidden in a cornfield near Maikop in 1942.

In North Africa in 1942, the observer watched his shots from the firing position.

In oppressive heat, Romanians and Germans observe the enemy in order to attack identified targets together at once, Romania, spring 1944.

The lieutenant with his VB radio set accompanies the heavy machine gun group of the spearhead into action.

An advanced observer in Lapland, December 1942.

Despite his wounds, this advanced observer continues to direct his battery's fire.

The artillery communications officer of AR 218, in contact with the surrounded "Battle Group Scherer" in Cholm, successfully directs, from inside, the fire of the batteries outside against the attacking enemy.

Artillery fire opened the campaigns on May 10, 1940 and June 22, 1941.

Preparatory fire along the Bug on June 22, 1941.

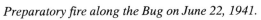

Artillery is not evaluated according to its position, but rather its effect. This is a shot-down Russian battery of 7.62 cm Div.Kan. 39.

Heavy artillery hit these tanks in their readiness position.

Above: Barrage Fire Area 132 of AR 263 near Staritzy, March 1944.
Below: Firefall south of Leningrad, summer 1943.

Two ammunition units supply the firing positions of the AR 263 batteries, even in areas deep in snow, in Russia, winter 1941.

Ammunition shortage is chiefly a transportation problem, as well as one of raw materials and production. The positions are being supplied before an attack at Kursk in 1943.

In the ice and snow, transporting ammunition, even within the firing position, demands superhuman effort.

In trackless country – here in France, after the June 1944 invasion – cannoneers carry 15 cm shells to their howitzer.

During an attack south of Ilmen Lake in March 1942, the two mountain units of Artillery Regiment 5 proved to be particularly mobile off the road.

There were mountain guns in the light, later Jäger, divisions and the mountain divisions. Their small caliber was made up for by their mobility. The 7.5 cm Geb.Kan. 36 (made by Rheinmetall) weighed 750 kg and fired 9.25 kilometers at a maximum elevation of 70 degrees. It is seen here before firing.

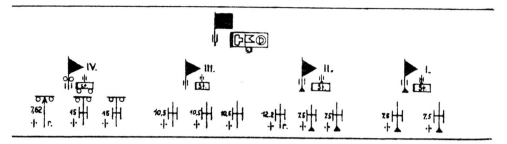

The composition of the artillery regiment of a Jäger or mountain division, here AR 81, 97th Jäger Division. The first two units otherwise had three batteries of mountain guns, the fourth had a 10 cm cannon battery. The captured guns were improvisations.

A pack column carries a mountain gun separated into eight loads through Finnish Lapland in December 1942.

The barrel of a mountain gun is carried by a mule.

A Mountain Cannon 36 of the 1st Mountain Division near Mount Elbruz in the Caucasus in August 1942; its position at an altitude of 4300 meters had no military value.

A mountain battery of 13 men and a gun changes positions in Lapland in the winter of 1942-1943.

Mountain guns fire at night in Lapland.

The 3rd unit of a mountain artillery regiment often used the leFH 16 n.A. instead of the leFH 18. Above: A battery changing positions in Lapland, summer 1943. Below: A leFH 16 mounted on a sturdy sled in the winter of 1942-1943.

During the costly retreats that began in December 1941, and again in the winter of 1942, increasing numbers of heavy horsedrawn artillery were lost.

The heavy 12./AR 263 in retreat near Burinovo-Novo Slobodka, southwest of Moscow, on December 25, 1941.

Light Field Howitzer 18 units of the Army Group North in retreat in 1944.

AR 263 in a snowstorm south of Malojaroslavez in 1941, with heavy demands on man and beast.

Firing positions on the closest interception line, here leFH 18 with muzzle brakes but wooden wheels.

Then on to the next defensive position, February 1944.

The crew enjoys a hot meal once a day.

The German border is reached in 1944.

The end comes along the Oder on February 22, 1945; after a cold, wet night the cannoneers dry their socks over a small fire in the morning.

For street fighting, firing on bunkers or at tanks, single guns were often moved forward for firefights. In times of crisis, cannoneers had to function as rifle companies, with heavy losses.

The leFH 18/40 on antitank mount, with strengthened muzzle brake, on December 8, 1944. In 1945, only 47% of artillery losses could be replaced.

Motor Vehicles

Before mounting, the cannoneers fold the spars; the ground spurs are already folded up – North Africa, 1941.

The 3-ton towing tractor (HKl 6), SdKfz 11, is already beginning the withdrawal, the work of minutes. Then in one hour it covers a day's march of a horsedrawn battery, quite apart from North Africa.

The 3-ton towing tractor was the artillery's lightest towing vehicle.

The 5-ton towing tractor (BN 9), SdKfz 6, with leFH 18, advancing in Russia on July 11, 1941, was extremely robust and reliable, and if necessary, it could tow two guns.

A 5-ton towing tractor near Rimini, Italy, in 1944.

The 8-ton towing tractor (KMm 11), SdKfz 7, in northern Russia in September 1943, towing an 8.8 cm Pak 43/41, range 15.3 km, spreading rather than cross mount, spars of the light field howitzer, wheels of the heavy howitzer, used as of late 1943 by various divisions, such as the III./AR 178, but not very successfully. Below: ideal structure of the artillery regiment (mot) of Panzergrenadier Division 44; it was actually smaller.

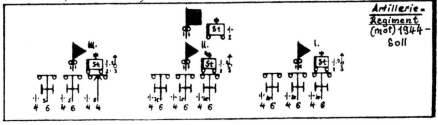

58

A heavy howitzer battery with 12-ton towing tractors clears out a field position of Italian 10.5 cm M 42 field guns in North Africa, December 1941.

The III./AR (mot) 74 of the 2nd Panzer Division rolls through the rubble of half-destroyed Sedan, France after the breakthrough in May 1940. The halftrack vehicles had been developed by the Reichswehr since 1933.

The 12-ton towing tractor (DB 10), SdKfz 8, with sFH 18 (mot), weight 6.3 tons, with barrel in marching position, towing capacity 12-14 tons, 11 seats, in southern Russia in 1942.

The heavy field howitzer (mot) seen stopped on the Mius, southern Russia, in March 1943. The heavy howitzer units (mot), whether uniform or mixed with a 10 cm gun battery, represented the mass of mobile army artillery used in forming focal points.

Raupenschlepper Ost (R 80/81 Steyr), used since 1942, with leFH 18/40 with improved muzzle brake, on the march near Kursk in 1943. The RSO pulled two tons, had a marching speed of 17 kph, and had only two seats, hence the limber being towed. The howitzer on antitank-gun spars weighed only 1.8 tons, but had elevation and traverse controls, and trigger at left by the aiming gunner. Its axle had double torsion bar suspension with a spread mount. The battery was 44 men less than a motorized battery in peacetime.

The heavy Wehrmacht towing tractor (SWS), Büssing-NAG, introduced in 1943, with 12 seats, 27 kph, 8-ton towing capacity, used by a sFH unit near Kursk in 1943.

The barrel of the sFH is moved from marching into firing position by the crew. This was considerably easier and quicker than with the heavy horsedrawn howitzer. Next the gun will be dismounted.

After the SWS drives away, the heavy field howitzer is shifted so its six tons are balanced and turned in the general firing direction.

"Firing pause" of a sFH battery near Kursk in 1943. Shells and cartridges are ready, and a gunner waits with the rammer for the shot. The mount axle (left) unburdens the towing hook of the tractor. Motorization spares personnel, provides tenfold mobility and extends the radius of action.

A heavy field howitzer of the III./PzAR 76 (6th PD) near Systevka in April 1942, to support the attack with the front turned toward the west.

A heavy howitzer battery in action near Arcoma in 1942.

Heavy field howitzers of the III./PzAR 76 firing near Nikite on March 23, 1942, during the relief attack on Sychevka.

Setting the fuse of a heavy howitzer shell in Poland, September 1939.

Cleaning a heavy field howitzer's barrel and riflings in Russia, April 1944.

In 1943 the paratroop artillery received recoilless light guns, which were dropped in four loads of 124 to 189 kg, plus the wheels. Pulled by the muzzle of the barrel, they had only a shortened box mount with a ground spur. They were used by Light Artillery Units (mot) 423, 424, 426, 429 and 430.

While loading the 10.5 cm light gun, the bag-shaped jet was swung to the side to clear the barrel.

The 7.5 cm LG 40, L/15.5, without a shield, fired eight shots per minute in roundabout fire from a tripod, with a range of 6.8 km. Firing was done from the side here. For a long period, the caliber was too small.

A 10.5 cm light gun of the 6th SS Mountain Division "Nord" in Lapland. In mountain use it fired high-angle fire.

A 15 cm Cannon 39 being turned in Russia in 1944. It had an 8.25-meter barrel, weighed 12.2 tons, was carried in three loads, and fired 24.8 kilometers. Its elevation went up to 45 degrees. As a field gun, it had a spread mount, otherwise an anchored ground plate allowing roundabout fire, a modern design. Without motor vehicles, these weapons could not have been used in the field.

A battery of 15 cm Cannon 39 guns is placed in positions near Wyasma and aimed on an October morning in 1941.

The 17 cm cannon in a mortar mount, along with the 21 cm mortar, formed the backbone of the army artillery. The barrel, 8.53 meters long, is seen here at 50-degree elevation. It weighed 17.5 tons, and its range was 29.6 km with an initial velocity of 925 meters per second.

Above: a 17 cm cannon about to be fired near Leningrad on December 29, 1942.
Below: the barrel of the 21 cm Cannon 39 (Krupp) rolls forward to a new position in 1940.

The 9.53-meter barrel of the 21 cm Cannon 39 of Army Artillery Unit (mot) 767 or 768, advancing 100 kilometers from Moscow in November 1941, was one of three loads of the 48.2-ton gun. With an initial velocity of 800 m/sec, it fired 30 km at 45-degree elevation. It could traverse 360 degrees.

A two-gun battery of 21 cm Cannon 38 fires in defensive action against the 1944 invasion in France. The 11.62-meter barrel fired 120-kilogram shells up to 33.9 kilometers.

One of the best designs by the Krupp designers who produced the 17 cm cannon and 21 cm mortar was the 21 cm Cannon 38, unfortunately dropped by Hitler. In firing position it weighed 25.3 tons, could be raised and lowered without a crane, and had double recoil. By 1943, seven of them had been built. Its rate of fire was 25 rounds per hour, its maximum elevation was 50 degrees.

The very laborious use of heavy guns with long-range effect, demanded by the enemy's ever-greater marching depth, was surpassed, step by step, by the development of rockets and made superfluous. Bomber aircraft had already limited their use.

The mount of a 21 cm mortar of the III./AR 288 (18th Artillery Division) is brought in by its towing tractor. The cannoneers begin their many jobs.

The barrel wagon has driven up to the mount, which was lowered onto the ground plate. Now the cannoneers use a winch to pull the 6.5-meter barrel out.

The 21-cm mortar is prepared for firing. The breech is open, the loading tray with the shell, which could scarcely be carried, is at hand.

The box mount of the 61.7-ton mortar is turned on the ground plate with the help of rollers after being guided in by the gunner to correct the coarse traverse setting – July 15, 1944.

The last preparations of the mortar, raised to 50 degrees. It was actually a two-load mortar-howitzer and could be elevated to 70 degrees. Russia, 1943-1944.

Two men raise the 6.51-meter barrel. After lowering, the aluminum wheels and rubber tires could be folded up. Italy, April-May 1944.

A 21-cm morter breech grenade being spring- loaded into a concrete shell. The ammunition gunners set the fuse.

The shell, weighing 113 or 121.4 kilograms, is lifted from the loading tray by the whole crew and inserted into the barrel in its horizontal loading position.

A 21 cm mortar firing. The K 2 opens the breech, and the next round is ready.

After the barrel is lowered, a cannoneer removes the hot cartridge.

A mortar battery firing.

Peacetime training with maneuver cartridges – battery firing in central Russia, February 1944.

A mighty blast and a huge ball of fire show the power unleashed in firing the 24 cm Skoda howitzer near Sevastopol, as later before Leningrad. As used by the II./AR 84, it was transported in two loads and weighed 8.6 tons in firing position. The shell weighed 127 kg. Despite its old-fashioned design, the gun was essential.

A morning alarm at the firing position of a battery of 24 cm Skoda Cannon (t) M 16, in mounts of the 38 cm howitzer, in 1940 during the western campaign. In 1938-39 twelve of these guns were taken over from the Czechs and moved in four loads. In firing position, a gun weighed 45.2 tons; with an initial velocity of 850 m/sec, it fired its 180 kg shells up to 32 kilometers.

The 28 cm Krupp L/12 Howitzer weighed 50.3 tons and had a range of 10.4 km. Here it is firing 350 kg explosive shells at night near Sevastopol in 1942.

The Skoda 30.5 cm Mortar was old-fashioned but certainly very effective.

*The Skoda M 17 42 cm Howitzer, L/
15, unlike the corresponding Krupp
design, continued to play a role in
World War II.*

*The loading winch of the 60 cm
"Karl" mortar lifts the concrete
shell, 2.5 meters long and weighing
2.117 tons, onto the sliding rollers
of the automatic loading apparatus
during the 1944 Warsaw uprising.
The shell could penetrate 4 meters
of armor plate.*

The heaviest German mortar – one of six – was also the heaviest German tracked vehicle, weighing 120 tons overall. Here it is firing at Warsaw in August 1944. During electric firing, the cylinder rods of the two barrel recuperators became visible. The 16-man crew could fire six shots per hour. Despite its dimensions: length 11.15 meters, width 3.15 m, height 4.78 m, it had a ground pressure of only 1.8 kg/sq. cm. The upper mount had double recoil with 580-ton braking pressure for the 30.5-ton barrel and 69.15-ton mount.

After the anti-aircraft artillery, on Göring's orders, had become part of the Luftwaffe in 1935, but could not strengthen air protection in the field by 1940, Army anti-aircraft units were established anew in the autumn of 1940, most of them at 4th units of motorized artillery or armored artillery regiments in 1941-1942. Then they became independent troops of the divisions, and a separate service arm in 1944. The unit had two heavy batteries, each with 4 to 6 8.8 cm, three 2 cm and two light machine guns, plus one light battery with six 3.7 cm guns, three self-propelled 2 cm quads, four 60 cm anti-aircraft searchlights and four light machine guns.

An army anti-aircraft gun with a shield for ground combat guards the advance of the "Grossdeutschland" Division between the Tim and Don during the attack on Woronesh in June 1942. The anti-aircraft units were used more and more as heavy antitank forces.

In the attack on the bridgehead south of Amiens and against the Weygand Line in 1940, the 9th Panzer Division mounted 8.8 cm anti-aircraft guns on 12-ton towing tractors for quick defense during costly action against the hard-fighting enemy.

From October 1943 to the end of January 1944, the Army Flak Artillery Unit 287 supported the 9th Panzer Division in the fight for the Nikopol bridgehead and prevented the Russians from prevailing.

This Army flak battery fired shot after shot against low-level Russian fighter planes on December 2, 1944.

Before changing positions on February 17, 1945, the heavily used barrels of the anti-aircraft guns are given a cleaning.

The launcher also came from the artillery and later became independent. This is a 15 cm sextuple unit 41 being loaded with shells that weighed over 30 kilograms. Artillery regiments of the Waffen-SS usually had one launcher battery.

Installing a Heavy Launcher Device 41, with 28 or 32 cm explosive or incendiary shells fired from packing cases, in northern France in 1944.

Heavy missiles in flight during the 1944 Warsaw uprising.

Reconnaissance Artillery

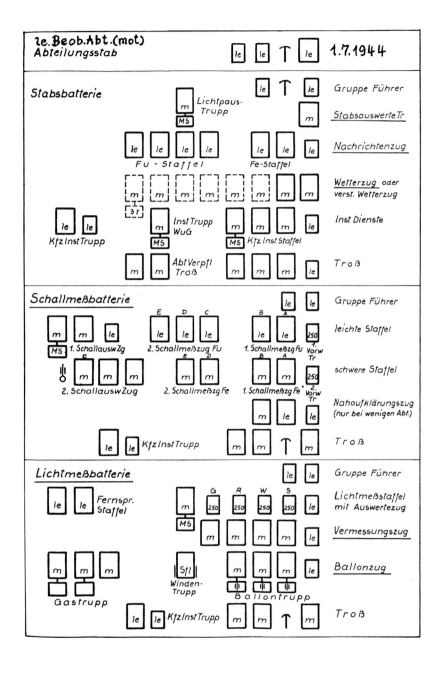

The measuring platoon
first calculates the
measuring positions of the
sound- and light-measur-
ing batteries by distance
with theodolites, plus a
notator. Otherwise all the
distances would be
indefinite. The measuring
batteries of the army
operated similarly.

Calculations are made on
the map of the light-
measuring batteries. The
artillery fire begins next.

How the sound-measuring
of an enemy battery leads
to targeting –right: sound
location of the target on
the oscillographs. A target
is often pinpointed by
sound and light.

Auswertung

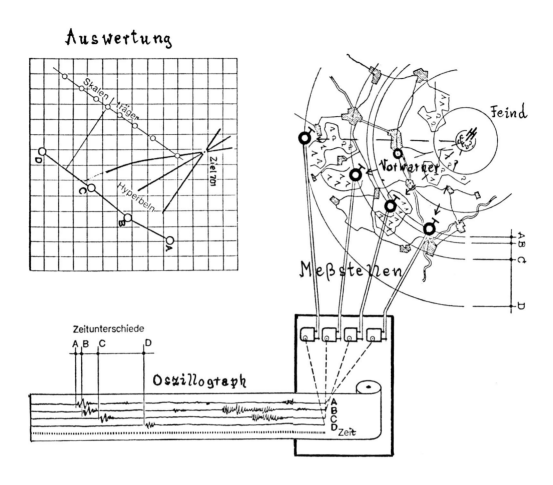

Skalen Träger

Ziel 701

Hyperbeln

D
C
B
A

Feind

Vorwarner

Meßstellen

A B C D

Zeitunterschiede

A B C D

Oszillograph

A
B
C
D
Zeit

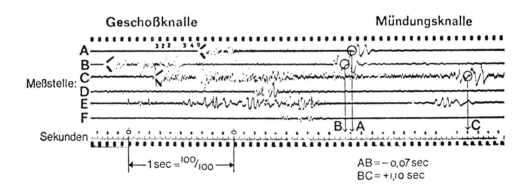

Geschoßknalle   Mündungsknalle

Meßstelle:
A
B
C
D
E
F

Sekunden

|← 1 sec = $^{100}/_{100}$ →|

AB = − 0,07 sec
BC = + 1,10 sec

Sound picture of a target located ahead of the right wing. It is the single shot of a cannon battery that is firing at Measuring Position C. Here the sound difference between the shot and muzzle sounds is greatest.

At the calculating position of the sound-measuring battery, the latest data of the sound pictures are immediately entered in the reconnaissance plan. The enemy's artillery location allows conclusions as to its intentions.

The weather platoon – only a troop in a Panzer Observation Battery – constantly measures the air temperature on the ground and in the air, and regularly gives the artillery the weather or "Barbara" report.

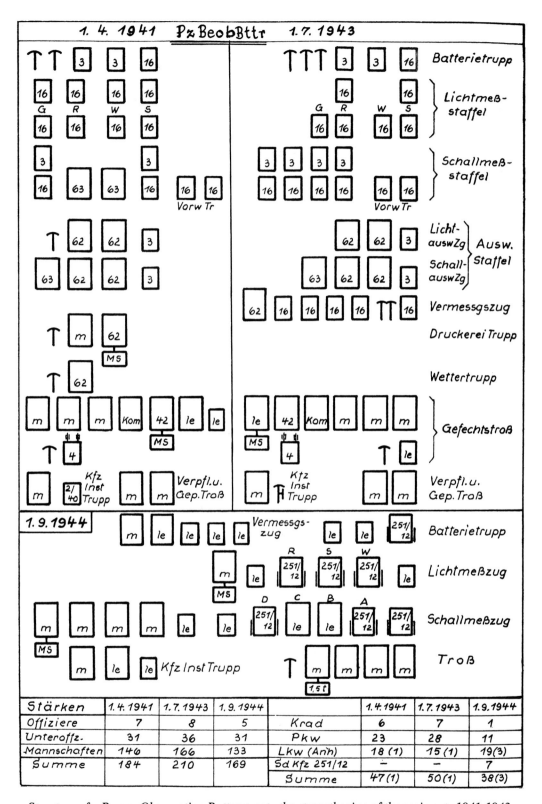

Stärken	1.4.1941	1.7.1943	1.9.1944		1.4.1941	1.7.1943	1.9.1944
Offiziere	7	8	5	Krad	6	7	1
Unteroffz.	31	36	31	Pkw	23	28	11
Mannschaften	146	166	133	Lkw (Anh)	18 (1)	15 (1)	19 (3)
Summe	184	210	169	Sd Kfz 251/12	–	–	7
				Summe	47 (1)	50 (1)	38 (3)

Structure of a Panzer Observation Battery; note the strengthening of the regiments 1941-1943.

A captive balloon (Type K) with 1500 cbm, with an observer, near Gomel in August 1941. The balloon battery had two balloons. They were filled with hydrogen gas, filled to 200 atmospheres by the gas echelon. The balloon was emptied for long-distance position changes.

The two observers in the basket wear aviation coveralls and parachutes for protection against coldness and wind. The observation height is between 600 and 1000 meters, or at most around 1500 meters.

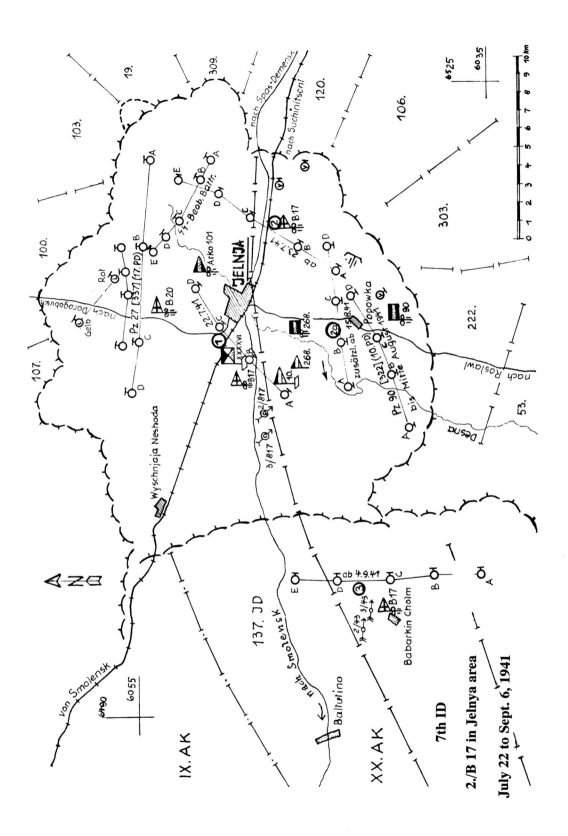

7th ID

2./B 17 in Jelnya area

July 22 to Sept. 6, 1941

95

Railroad Artillery

Railroad guns are very demanding and sensitive to air, but provide heavy surface fire with large calibers and ranges. There were also mortars mounted on railroad cars. Left: 20.3 cm Cannon (E) L/59 with 47-degree elevation and all-around fire. Six guns fell into Allied hands in France in 1944. Below: 24 cm Cannon (E) "Theodor Bruno" on the turntable while loading shells shortly before firing.

Left-flank fire of a 28 cm "Short Bruno" cannon battery (E) on the Channel coast of Belgium in 1944. The turntable used to turn the gun is clearly visible. The shrapnel protection is modest, while camouflage, air defense and close-range defense are lacking altogether.

The gunner aims the 28 cm cannon, while the K 2 switches on the breech safety near the trigger line.

Above: a look into the 28 cm cannon's mouth, showing inner barrel and jacket, to the open breech with the shell in place.
Below: Before firing the 28 cm Cannon (E) K 5, the crew hangs on, because of the air pressure.

The 28 cm Cannon (E) K 5 was the most modern, most successful and most numerous German railroad gun, developed since 1934, with 25 guns built by the war's end, some used by Batteries 712, 713 and 765. With rocket shells, ranges of 86.5 km were attained, and about 160 km with smaller-caliber shells.

The 28 cm K 5 of Instruction and Replacement for Railroad Artillery (mot) 100 in Rügenwalde, Pomerania, in the pine forests along the Baltic coast, at its greatest barrel elevation of 50 degrees. Here troop testing was carried out and evaluated by Oberstleutnant Reissmüller.

Four 52 cm mortar-howitzers (f) M 18, L/16 of 1918 were copied from the 42 cm mortar by Schneider-Creuzot, captured in France in 1940, and used at Leningrad in 1942-1943 and Warsaw in 1944. The 30-meter gun weighed 265 tons, and a barrel 8.35 meters long and weighing 45 tons. The explosive shells (above) of 1.37 and 1.42 tons had ranges of 17.5 and 18 km.

The muzzle of the inner barrel of the 80 cm "Dora" Cannon (E). Below: the 80 cm "Dora" Cannon (E) on two tracks, fenced in and camouflaged, with two ammunition lifts in the rear. The gun is mounted on two railroad cars.

The 80 cm "Dora" Cannon – the world's largest gun.

Artillery Structure of the 17th Army

As of 9/3/1943

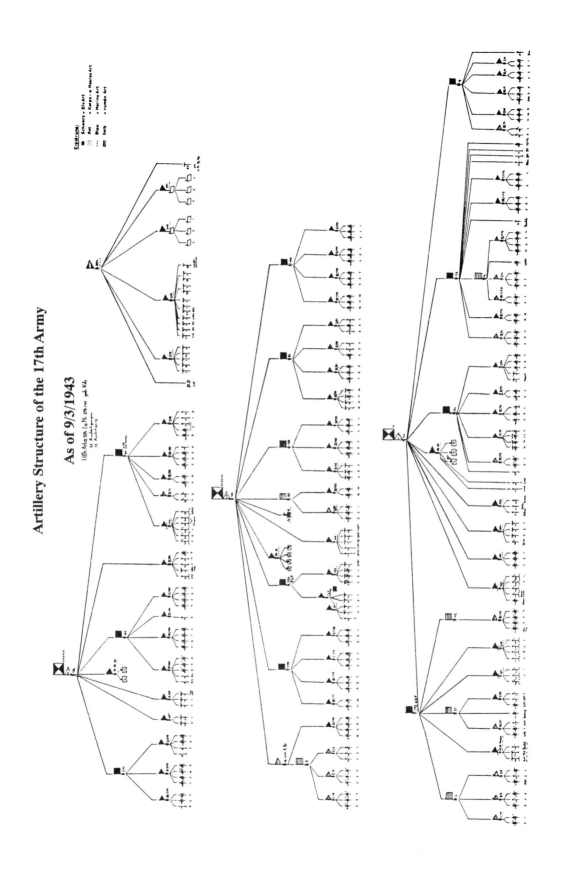

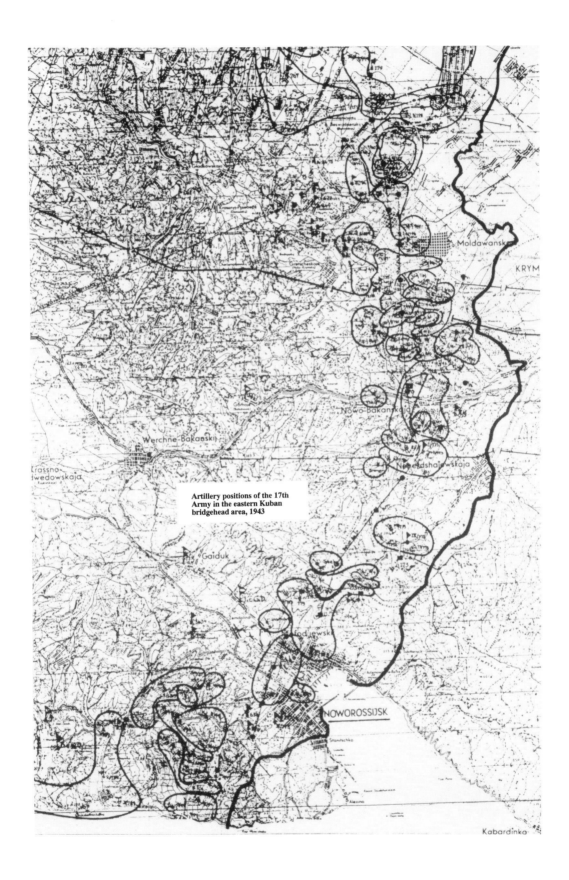

Artillery positions of the 17th Army in the eastern Kuban bridgehead area, 1943

ARTILLERY COMMAND AT HOME AND IN THE FIELD
INSPECTOR OF THE ARTILLERY
WITH CHIEF ARMY EQUIPMENT & COMMANDER, REPLACEMENT ARMY

General of the Coast and Fortress Artillery: General of the Army, Anti-Aircraft Troops, General of the Artillery with Commander West, High Officer for Panzer Artillery, High Officer of the Observation Troops, General of the Fog Troops

Weapons Schools	Artillery Inspection Army	Weapons Office
Art. Schools I-III Assault Art. School 6 other Weapon Schools Artillery Schools I-III of the Waffen-SS	(In 4) in A.H.A. with Groups I-III Reserve Art. Regt. Art. Repl. Regt.	Groups for Artillery, Developing & Testing, Ind. Equipment, Special Weapons
	Training Replacement Establishment Armament Weapon Development Advising Reporting	

**Reserve,
Replacement & Training Units
of the
Replacement Army**

GENERAL OF THE ARTILLERY
WITH COMMANDER OF THE ARMY, LATER IN O.K.H./O.K.W.

**General of the Artillery – Army Group
High Artillery Commander/Sto.Art. – Army
Artillery Commander – Army Corps
Regimental Commander – Division** (Division Artillery Commander)

Artillery Planning, Command, Replacement
Tactics (Evaluation of Experience)
Firing Procedures
Reconnaissance Artillery
Ammunition Supply
Measurement
Maps
Weather Service

**Units
of the
Field Army**

The organization commanding the army at home, like its command hierarchy in the field, from the General of the Artillery in the Army High Command to the units, had to represent determination and willingness to fight on the lower level. There was good reason for the "Artillery Assault Medal." Many received the Infantry Close Combat Bar in bronze, Honor Roll Bar, German Cross in gold, and higher decorations. Here are a few examples to represent many unnamed:

The Chief of the 11./A.R. 178 (78th Assault Division), Oberleutnant Harprecht, supported with his heavy howitzer battery, on the morning of July 26, 1941, the procedure of the I./I.R. 195 against the dominating Height 193. When he advanced ahead of the infantry and encountered Russians who were trying to seize the important height just then, it became clear to him at once what possession of the height meant in the framework of the total situation, how decisive its possession in the face of the enemy was, and how meager his chances for successful resistance appeared. Without delay, he radioed his IVth Unit: "Situation requires concentrated fire on Height 193!" Shortly after that he fell under the fire of his own guns; the enemy withdrew.

As of July 11, 1943, the 3rd Soviet Panzer Army burst forth east of Orel for a counteroffensive against the German operations on Kursk with superior forces. The advanced 36th I.D. (mot.) was deployed on the left wing of the 262nd I.D./XXXV. Army Corps, along with A.R. (mot.) 36, which was strengthened by a 21 cm mortar unit, not far from the Ssusha. The terrain channeled the attacking space of the enemy, for the destruction of which the Regimental Commander, Oberstleutnant Dinkelaker, prepared the fire zone "Hammer." On July 14 the enemy attacked Shelyabug with 550 tanks. The unified regiment fired until the barrels became hot. At Target Point 147 sat Lt. Schmitz, II./A.R. (mot.) 36, as advanced observer. He let the Panzer Army roll over his position and

directed fire from within the mass of the enemy, which attacked in regimental columns. The commander spoke with him; he knew what would happen. "To all. Concentrate fire on Point 147, Schmitz observed, in two minutes – now!" Schmitz's corrections required hasty decisions. The regiment fired for hours in full; the enemy could not back off. Schmitz and his radioman still crouched in their foxhole, although there had been no German infantry there for hours. After 40 Russian tanks had been shot down, the other 400 turned away to bring their infantry forward again. In addition, several fighters and dive-bombers appeared. At 1630 hours, Lt. Schmitz no longer answered. The next morning he and his radioman were found, killed by a tank shell. Oberst Dinkelaker received the Knight's Cross on December 9, 1943.

The decreasing battle strength of the infantry compelled many divisions to use cannoneers, as well as antitank forces and supply personnel as infantrymen, more than thirty times in the case of A.R. (mot.) 18, for example. Overextended battle lines with gaps led to crisis situations.

On August 12, 1943, 20 kilometers east of Jarzewo, Oberleutnant Tiepolt, Chief, 4./A.R. (mot.) 18, received orders from his division to take a patch of woods and then an important hill along his neighbor's line on the highway to Dorogobusch in the open flank of Panzer Grenadier Regiment 51, and to hold them until relieved by reinforcements. With 90 cannoneers without any heavy weapons he advanced after a firefall, but was surprised by being fired on himself, encountered tanks, yet pushed ahead with twelve men to the attack target, two men being wounded. For more than three days he held the important position without any communication, until relieved by the 1st and 2nd/P.G.R. 51. Since they had been listed as "missing", they received neither ammunition nor rations. Of his cannoneers, 18 more men later made their way to the command post. A week later, Smolensk fell. On October 10, 1943, Tiepolt received the "German Cross in Gold."

In the morning twilight of October 16, 1941, Oberleutnant Engelmann, Chief, 4./ A.R. (mot.) 18, crossed the Volchov, 300 meters wide, in rubber boats as the advanced observer with the 9./I.R. 426 as the spearhead company of the 126th I.D., in order to support the formation of a bridgehead with the IInd Unit to advance on Mal. Vischera. While stopping before the attack on Ljubivzevo, which was to proceed, late in the afternoon, far across coverless turnip fields toward a wooded coulisse, despite the suspicious stillness, he offered to Major Bunzel, Commander, III./I.R. 426, to go between the fronts along to tempt the presumed enemy to come out. After head-shaking permission, the lone crier walked several hundred meters toward the woods, until finally a single Russian stood up, whom he greeted and amiably embraced. Then other individual figures rose up at the edge of the woods, more and more, a whole battalion within ten minutes, who threw down their weapons and came over. Without a shot being fired, the woods and village thus could be taken by evening, the bridgehead expanded and secured. The infantry suddenly had more prisoners than men; it was impossible to guard them or transport them away. The artilleryman was wounded during the night. A week later, Mal. Vischera was taken.

Like every service arm, artillerymen also had remarkable experiences in combat. Naturally, they were not exposed to the full extent of the actual combat as much as other combat troops were, although that changed more and more since the autumn of 1943, and indeed sometimes became the opposite as of 1944. Army artillery here today, there tomorrow – were always welcome arrivals, but were overlooked for advancement and decorations, because they were usually there too short a time and did not belong to the unit itself. Their accomplishments could not add up, their achievements belonged to the division on the combat front. They were independent birds of passage as "reinforcement artillery", and therefore more self-conscious and selfless in terms of needing recognition.

Quantities of Available Weapons, 1939-1945

Available Weapons on

	9/1/39	4/1/40	6/1/41	10/1/44	1/1/45
lFH 10.5 cm	4,845	5,381	7,076	6,592	8,059
sFH 15 cm	2,049	2,330	2,867	2,521	3,000
10 cm Cannon	702	700	760	550	714
21 cm Mortar	22	124	388	?	218*

*8 On 3/1/1945.

Source: Wa I Rü. WaStabSt/No. 600/45 g/Kdos. "Überblick über den Rü.Stand des Heeres" of 3.1.1945.

Notes:

1. Available weapons are those on hand with the troops and in the area of the Ordnance Inspection.

2. The numbers of available weapons on 1/1/1945 differ from those that result when one adapts the figures for 1/1/1944 on the basis of losses and production according to Table 68, going up or down somewhat. These differences are explained by late reports of consumption figures, which, particularly in the last year of the war, were to be expected on account of the hasty pace of events.

From July 1941 to November 1941, production just equaled losses. As of December 1941, production fell behind losses. Whereas there were still 140 light and 50 to 60 heavy howitzers produced in April 1941, by December of that year there were only 21 light and 10 heavy ones. Still in all, the direction of production, ammunition supply by the Army Weapons Office, as well as supplying of the artillery, were great organizational achievements.

Quantities, Consumption and Production of Weapons, 1941-1942

	Quantity on 6/1/41	Consumption 12/41-2/42	Production 1/42	Quantity on 2/1/42
lFH 16 & 18 (10.5 cm)	7,076	147	0	6,155
sFH 13 & 18 (15 cm)	2,867	361	9	2,514
Mortar 18 (21 cm)	388	32	0	404

Notes:

1. "Quantity" is the number of weapons received from industrial production and turned over to the army ordnance department.

2. "Consumption" is the loss in any manner in the entire field and replacement armies including supplies to other countries.

3. The consumption figure of 147 lFH is presumably incorrect. The consumption from 6/22/1941 to 3/15/1942 was 1,307.

Quantities in Army Artillery Units

Quantity	9/1/1939	4/1/1940	6/20/1941
Light Howitzer	4,845	5,381	7,076
Heavy Howitzer	2,049	2,330	2,867
10 cm Cannon	325	475	760
21 cm Mortar	22	124	388
Assault Gun	5	6	377

	6/1/1941	7/1/1942	7/1/1942	4/13/1944
sFH	38	32	23	138
10 cm Cannon	31	26	20	(Note: includes
gem. Abt.	12	12	12	light Army AA &
21 cm Mortar	30	26	21	coast artillery
Army Coast Artil.	173	415	513	units.)

Total Production	1940	1941	1942	1943	1944
Guns (7.5 cm & up)	6,100	7,200	12,000	27,250	41,500
Artillery ammunition (in millions)	25	27	59	94	109.3

The final decrease in **weapon** production began in December 1944, in **ammunition** as of September 1944.

Howitzer Production, second half of 1944

	Monthly Average 44	Sept. 44	Oct. 44	Nov. 44	Dec. 44
lFH	839	638	925	919	1,082
sFH	252	308	264	315	301

Total Supplies of Artillery Guns

	January 1945	February 1945
Total number	1,225	665
for Field Army	74%	71%
by piece	907	473

Source: Engelmann, "Deutsche Artillerie 1934 bis 1945", Starke Publishing, Limburg.

GUN LOSSES

	5/10-6/20/1940	On Hand 6/1/1941	12/1/41-2/28/1942	Supplied 6/22/1941-3/15/1942	Oct-Dec 1944
lFH	137	7,076	1,307*	537	1,091
sFH	88	2,867	361	350	388
21 cm Mortar	6	388	32	–	72

* (6/22/1941-3/15/1942)

The loss of guns through damage and material wear totals 7,184 by 6/20/1941. The general loss rate for the eastern army was 11% as of August 31, 1941, but rose to 23.5% by November 26, 1941. Correspondingly, weapon losses also increased considerably. In the second half of 1944 they were:

	12/1/1943-6/30/1944	7/31/1944	9/30/1944	10/31/1944	11/30/1944
Assault Gun	1,486	170	290	493	2,409
lFH (sf)	166	209	232	253	257
sFH (sf)	111	181	206	228	240

	5/1/1943-4/30/1944	7/31/1944	9/30/1944	10/31/1944	11/30/1944
lFH	249	–	389	648	272
percentage			60.9%	70.0%	29.6%
sFH	93	–	157	220	80
percentage			50.9%	83.3%	25.4%

Note: Highest losses of **lFH** 1,170 (8/44), of **sFH** 382 (7/44).

Production and Consumption of Weapons, October 1944-February 1945

Weapon	Month	Produced	Consumed	Sold or Given Away	Total Consumption
lFH 10.5 cm	10/44	785	648	54	703
	11/44	909	278	38	316
	12/44	930	165	15	180
	1/45	364	208	0	208
	2/45	150	760	0	760
sFH 15 cm	10/44	264	220	4	224
	11/44	315	97	4	101
	12/44	208	71	0	71
	1/45	232	61	6	67
	2/45	155	324	1	325
21 mm Mortar	10/44-2/45	17	72	0	72

Against the advice of the industry and the Army Weapons Office, Hitler, as supreme commander of the Wehrmacht, expressly ordered in 1940 that ammunition production be cut back, with the result that from June 1941 to March 1942 the supply of artillery ammunition was reduced by one-third from increased consumption of ammunition, and the fighting strength of the artillery was considerably weakened. Only 15 months later was this shortage compensated for! As of January 1941, the percentage of artillery ammunition in the whole production of ammunition was reduced from 27% to 7% by December 1941.

While there were still 700,000 rounds of light howitzer shells produced in February 1941, in December of that year only 9,000 rounds were made, while 1.26 million were consumed. There were 49,000 heavy howitzer shells produced in December 1941, but 333,200 used. The fact that production remained about the same despite the vast expansion of the war in 1941 was an irremediable error! In terms of organization and raw materials, the industry was overextended.

Consumption, Production and Supplies of Ammunition, 1941-1942
(numbers = 1000 rounds)

	lFH 10.5 cm		sFH 15 cm		10 cm Cannon		21 cm Mortar	
	-	+	-	+	-	+	-	+
5/10-6/20/1940 (Western Campaign)	1463	1110	640	280	249	137	15,8	33
June 1941		50		212		21		33
August		1		121		7		13
October	1592	124	426	39	128	6	29	12
November	839	158	245	199	60	6	4	4
December	1272	105	338	88	109	4	12	4
January 1942	1777	168	311	100	77	4.6	14	4
February	1414	319	352	204	70	4	15	8
March	1803	343	425	223	120	9	21	11
April	1182	698	354	264	90	46	21	14
May	1127	1166	316	327	81	75	25	19
June	1542	1814	476	425	130	70	55	18
July	1173	2041	414	491	100	72	20	22
August	1721	2110	420	586	92	71	26	23

| On hand | 4/1/40 | 18,970 | | 3,813 | | 1,427 | | 96,5 | |
| | 6/1/41 | 25,799 | | 5,811 | | 2,580 | | 464 | |

| Low point | | 5/1/1942 | | 7/1/1942 | | 9/1/1942 | | 4/1/1942 | |
| | | 9,721 | | 1,136 | | 1,558 | | 316 | |

- = consumption; + = production

112

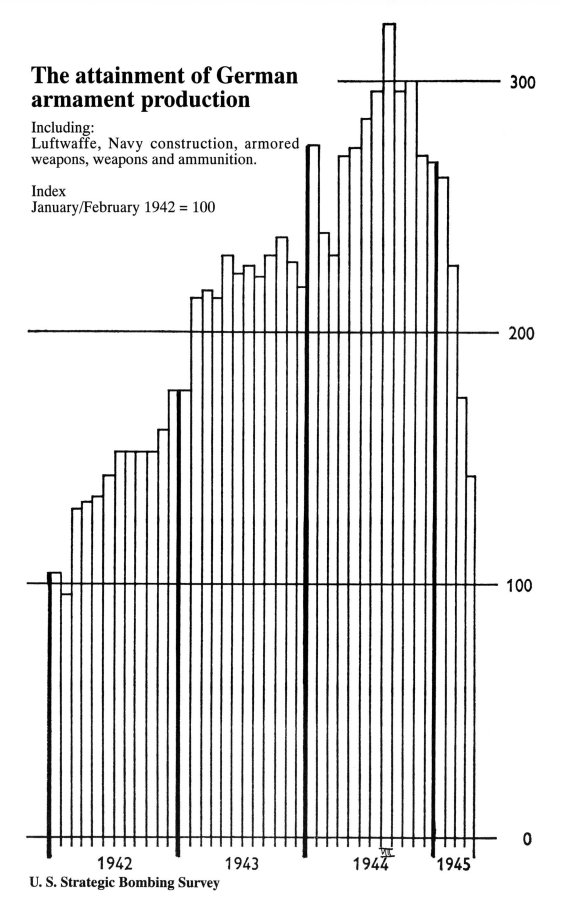

The attainment of German armament production

Including:
Luftwaffe, Navy construction, armored weapons, weapons and ammunition.

Index
January/February 1942 = 100

300

200

100

0

1942   1943   1944   1945

U. S. Strategic Bombing Survey

113

Self-propelled Mounts

A battery officer of Assault Gun Unit 184, in central Russia in 1941, shouts: "Gun crew, get ready!" from the open hatch of the shear telescope, the antenna raised. The casemate howitzer with shortened trajectory was infantry escort artillery, neither armored nor heavy antitank gun! Lack of antitank weapons lead to the installation of a cannon with step-by-step doubling of the barrel length. The "Hummel" and "Bison" assault howitzers remained the actual assault guns, while most of the Panzerjäger troops were equipped with assault guns in 1944-1945.

Type A of the 1940 assault gun used by Manstein during the first action in France, with the short 7.5 cm howitzer, L/24, nicknamed "Stummel" (stump), with double light infantry-gun barrel.

The Assault Gun 40 with the 7.5 cm L/43 gun with muzzle brake, seen south of Staraya Russa in the spring of 1942 during the "Winterreise" attack of the Seydlitz Group to open the Demjansk Pocket.

Assault Gun Battery

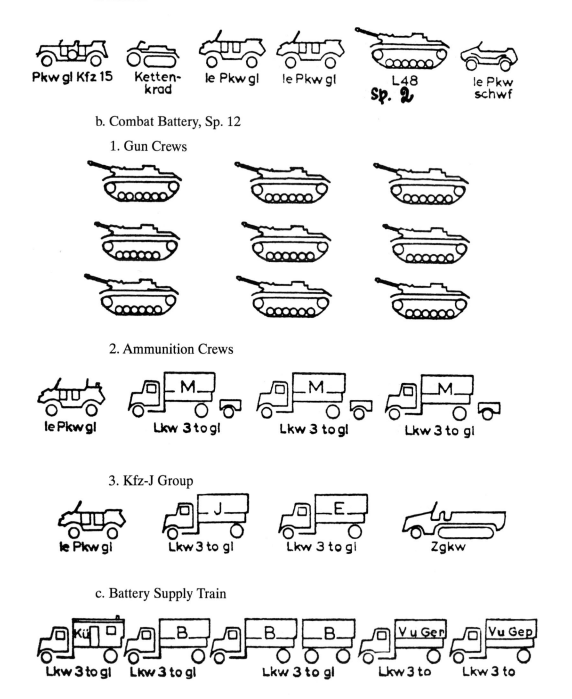

a. Leader

Pkw gl Kfz 15   Ketten-krad   le Pkw gl   le Pkw gl   L48 Sp. 2   le Pkw schwf

b. Combat Battery, Sp. 12

1. Gun Crews

2. Ammunition Crews

le Pkw gl   Lkw 3 to gl   Lkw 3 to gl   Lkw 3 to gl

3. Kfz-J Group

le Pkw gl   Lkw 3 to gl   Lkw 3 to gl   Zgkw

c. Battery Supply Train

Lkw 3 to gl   Lkw 3 to gl   Lkw 3 to gl   Lkw 3 to   Lkw 3 to

Structure of an assault-gun battery with 10, later 14 guns, in a unit with three batteries. The assault-gun battery had the firepower of a horsedrawn artillery unit.

Assault Gun III with 7.5 cm gun L/48 and muzzle brake, securing a causeway on the Don before Woronesh, June 1942. Below: The same type with cradle armor, welded-on front plate and side aprons to repel hollow charges and cement coating to repel magnetic mines, resembled a tank more and more.

So it was planned in advance: assault guns lead the infantry into an attack in southern Russia in 1942 and wipe out nests of resistance.

The battery chief decorates cannoneers and a crew with the Iron Cross at Vitebsk on March 16, 1944, before the large-scale Soviet offensive at the end of June. 70% of all assault guns were in the East and in Italy in 1943, twice as many as were in the West. At the same time, their production was half again as great as tank production, in order to almost catch up by 1944.

Locations of Assault Guns, June 30, 1943

East	997
Finland/Norway	34
West	113
Southeast	56
Italy	222

Existing Assault Gun Units, April 13, 1944

Total 42, of which

East   34

in all: **100 assault gun and assault artillery brigades,**

15 independent batteries

An assault gun with 10.5 cm assault howitzer L.28 – precisely the leFH 18 M – with muzzle brake, machine-gun shield, "pig's-head" (saukopf) mount around the barrel attachment, and infantrymen aboard.

The turret of the Panzer II was replaced on the "Wespe" by a lightly armored open structure with the leFH 18/40. As of 1942, an improvised "antitank howitzer" was available as well. The crew consisted of the gun leader, driver and three cannoneers, who were also radioman and driver. This gun was never under armor.

With its ground clearance of 34.5 cm, the "Wespe" traveled off-road at 24 kph, spanned ditches up to 1.70 meters wide, climbed over obstacles up to 42 cm high, and climbed grades up to 40 degrees, technical advantages despite its too-meager weapon effectiveness.

The ammunition tank, seen here at a repair shop, carried 90 rounds. The "Wespe" had only 32 rounds on board.

The six-gun battery had two ammunition tanks. This gun is seen in Beauvais on its way to Paris.

Having reported ready to fire, the crew awaits the command to fire. The elevation is 42 degrees, the firing height 1.94 meters. The "Wespe" is 4.81 meters long, 2.28 meters wide and 2.30 meters high, and weighs 11 tons. Its front armor is 18 mm thick, that on the sides 15 mm.

The gun crews – with their readiness-position camouflage – ford a river on the way to their firing position. The combination of gun and tractor as a self-propelled mount had both advantages and disadvantages. The field of traverse was limited to 40 degrees.

The muzzle flash at night clearly shows the typical silhouettes of the gun and its crew. Immediately after firing, the battery left its position, which would have been easy to calculate, and remained difficult to track down.

Self-propelled Artillery Mount Production

1940	1941	1942	1943	1944	1945	Notes
–	–	1248	2557	1248	87	
				total 5140		
	–	16.0%	31.0%	60.0%	–	Includes Russian plus German production

PANZER-
ARTILLERIE
REGIMENT

STABS-BATTERIE   BEOBACHT. BTTR.

I.

STABS-BATTERIE   1. (SF.) BATTERIE [Wespe]   2. (SF.) BATTERIE [Wespe]   3. (SF.) BATTERIE [Hummel]

The Panzer Artillery Regiment (1944) had a manifold profile:

1st Unit: Armored Howitzer Unit with — 2 light armored howitzer batteries of 6 lFH 18/2 (Wespe (Sfl)
1 heavy armored howitzer battery of 6 sFH 18/1 Hummel (Sfl)

2nd Unit: 1 Howitzer Unit with — 2 light howitzer batteries of 6 lFH 18 (motZg) each, or
3 light howitzer batteries of 4 lFH 18 (motZg) each

3rd Unit: heavy howitzer unit mixed with — 2 heavy howitzer batteries of 4 sFH 18 (motZg) each
1 10 cm cannon battery of 4 Kan 18 (motZg)
The regiment had 42 guns. The armored observation battery consisted of one light-measuring, one sound-measuring and one weather platoon, plus a printing troop. Each battery had three armored observation vehicles.

After heavy fire, finally a pause at the firing position. Empty cartridges and cases lie all around. But the next shells are already ready.

A "Wespe" on the march overland, with spare track links on the nose. In one hour it could equal the daily performance of a horsedrawn battery.

Armored howitzers guard the retreat of the 8th Army – one of their most important types of action – at the edge of the Carpathian Mountains south of Kronstadt on August 24, 1944.

A typical picture of a "Wespe" battery in firing position, ready to fire and awaiting the command to fire, in the summer of 1943.

The advantages of mobility, off-road capability and quick readiness to fire still balanced the disadvantages of full armor at that time. The Panzer-Artillery regiments would have needed two units of them, the motorized artillery regiments one. Their development was limited by the few available chassis, and was limited to fully armored self-propelled mounts such as the "Bison" and "Brummbär."

Technical service to a 15 cm "Hummel" battery behind the front.

A "Hummel" battery marches through a French city in 1944.

127

The gun crews march up to their firing positions – on the front since 1943. The armor plate measured 80 mm all around.

A battery often took up firing positions with too little space between guns, as their time spent there would be quite short in any case.

The sFH "Hummel" firing in Russia, in the winter of 1943-1944. Shells are standing ready on the cases of the propellant charges.

A look into the fighting compartment of the "Hummel" from the rear. At left is the gun leader with headphones and microphone, waiting for the battery officer's command to fire. Two cannoneers are just inserting the shell in the barrel.

A Waffen SS sFH (sf) with camouflage net, Gun Car III/IV, rolls ahead during the Ardennes offensive in December 1944. Below: 3./PzAr 75 of the 3rd Panzer Division in action.

The gun had a six-man crew, seen here in fatigues, reached 42 kph with a range on 215 km on and 130 km off the road. The muzzle of the barrel was 97 cm out and thus had to be supported. The vehicle was 6.20 meters long without the gun, 2.97 meters wide and 2.81 high. It was made by the Deutsche Eisenwerke in Duisburg and Deutsche Röhrenwerke in Mülheim. The small steel frame ahead of the driver's window aided him in orientation.

A "Hummel" battery changes position, moving forward. Thanks to their mobile self-propelled mounts, the Panzer artillery was always capable of following the attacking or flanking thrusts of the tanks closely and opening fire without delay without being essentially endangered by infantry combat.

The "Hummel" armored howitzer at its greatest elevation – very seldom used – as seen from below. The spare track links on the nose provided shrapnel protection.

The howitzer is loaded with shell and cartridge, thus ready to fire; the ordered elevation has been reached. With his raised hand, the gun leader reports to the battery officer that he is ready to fire. Gunner 2, near the barrel at right, waits for the command to pull the trigger.

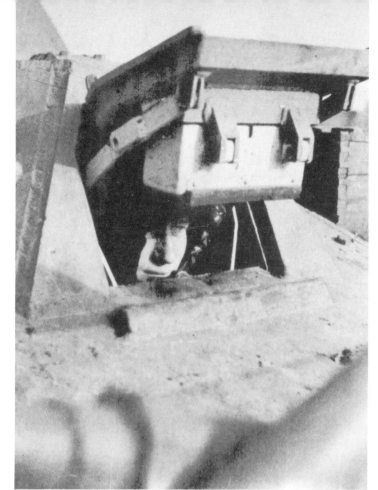

The driver, seen under the opened hatch with its heavy armor, and with a thick glass periscope inside.

At the Aachen front a "Hummel" battery receives ammunition for the Ardennes offensive on December 6, 1944.

Gunners 4 and 5 load the next shell. Gunner 2 has the cartridge ready. Under the rear entry door in the aiming grid, marked in red and white.

On captured French Lorraine tractors, a limited number of outmoded but usable sFH 13/1 guns were mounted by fitting the fighting compartment and adding a strong ground spur. The result was the improvised Special Vehicle 135/1.

Weapon Carrier II for the heavy infantry gun and sFH L/28, called "Sturmhaubitze 43", on the 638/20 gun car, a late attempt to create a 1945 uniform gun mount.

The Henschel short-range reconnaissance plane used by the Army's Panzer Corps units served the artillery observers for scouting as well as for targeting heavy artillery through air observation.

Above: 15 cm Howitzer 1/12 as "Bison", Type H (Sd.Kfz. 138/1), for the infantry gun companies of the Panzer Grenadier regiments. Below: The same howitzer in the Sturmpanzer IV "Brummbär" (Sd.Kfz. 166) completely under armor, an outstanding achievement, used by the troops since November 1943.

Left: The 28.2-ton "Brummbär", with skirts to protect it from hollow charges, advances in the August 1944 Warsaw uprising. The gun had a five-man crew, a top speed of 40 kph, and 38 shells on board. In all, 306 of them were built.

Below: The last version of the assault howitzer, with a machine gun in the ball mantelet and built-over driver's lookout, seen in Warsaw in 1944.

Fortress and Coast Artillery Immobile

A well-camouflaged 15 cm gun in the open West Wall area near Saarbrücken on April 30, 1940, six weeks before the Saar breakthrough.

The 15 cm Kanone 16, an outmoded model with insufficient performance, in an open firing position on the channel coast on October 16, 1941, a poor substitute for coastal batteries.

The 10.7 cm field gun (f/r) on the Adriatic coast in the summer of 1941, captured and used to secure open coastal positions.

In defending the coasts, the artillery needed range finders, like this one seen on the Norwegian Finnmark coast in 1942.

As of 1942, Russian guns were also used to guard the coasts. This is a 12.2 cm field gun (r) M 31, uncamouflaged and open on a makeshift pivot in southern France, during firing drill.

A 15 cm gun battery on the "Atlantic Wall" on June 19, 1943, camouflaged, to be sure, but still in an open firing position a year before the invasion.

Even this 28 cm gun battery just behind the dunes near Knokke, seen on June 1, 1943, was indefensible against air and sea superiority without concrete to protect it. In 1944 this coast was attacked, not from the sea but overland from the west.

Along the Atlantic coast there were guns from all over Europe, almost a museum. This leFH 16 is in an open position behind coastal barriers in northern France. Usually they lacked foglaying or close-range defensive equipment. Below: A 22 cm gun under heavy concrete, presumably near Dieppe, on March 4, 1944.

Long-Range Rockets

Above: The unfueled A4 rocket (V2) is brought out of the depot to the firing position by railroad. Below: before launching, the rocket is raised from the Meiller trailer to a vertical position, programmed and fueled, as here in Heimatartillerie-Park 11 at Peenemünde.

An A4 long-range rocket battery having its control system checked. The personnel needs for use of the V2 amounted to almost a division in 1944-1945.

The four-stage solid-fuel "Rheinbote" (V4) rocket developed by Prof. Heinrich Klein is being fired here by Army Artillery Unit (mot) 709 under OTL Tröller. At a maximum range of 160 kilometers it had the effect of fifteen 21 cm mortar shells, which promised it a great future.

Artillery Units

ARTILLERY INSTRUCTIONAL TROOPS

Art. Lehr Rgt. 1 (horse)	Instructional troop of the horsedrawn artillery at Jüterbog, Gross Born
Art. Lehr Rgt. 2 (mot)	Instructional troop of the light and heavy artillery (mot) for front service
Art. Lehr Rgt. 3 (mot)	Instructional troop of the observation artillery, balloon and measuring units at Jüterbog, Gross Born
Art. Lehr Rgt. 4 (mot)	Instructional Troop of the measuring and map troops at Gross Born, established August 14, 1943
Art. Lehr Rgt. 5	Instructional troop of the Panzer and motorized artillery at Gross Born
Sturm-Art. Lehr Abt./Brg.	from VI./Art. Lehr Rgt. Burg, near Magdeburg
H.-Flakart. Lehr Abt.	Instructional troop of the Army Flak Artillery, Perik, Schongau
Eisenbahnartillerie-Sch. Instructional	troop of the Railroad
Abt. (mot) 100	Artillery at Rügenwalde
H.-Küst.Art.LehrAbt 101	Instructional troop of the Army Coast Artillery at Rügenwalde, Agde
Art.Ausb-Abt. (t mot) 271	Instructional troop for special weapons at Schneidemühl
Fernraketen-Lehr- und Versuchs-Batterie 444	Peenemünde-Ost

German artillery on the move. The artillery used eight-horse hitches in heavy country, as here in the east in 1941.

Field Troop Units

Troop Unit (Artillery Regt.)		Replacement District	War Structure Subordination
(Pz.)Art.Rgt.(mot) GD		III	Pz.Gren.Div.GD Pz.K.GD
(Pz.)Art.Rgt.(mot) FHH		XX	Pz.Gren.Div.FHH Pz.K.FHH
(Pz.)Art.Rgt.(mot) Brandenburg		III	Pz.Gren.Div. Brandenburg
Art.Abt.(mot)FB		-	Für.Begl.Brig.
Pz.Art.Rgt.FG		-	Fü.Gren.Div.
	1	I	1.Inf.Div.
Reit.Art.Abt.	1	I	1.Kav.Brig.
Reit.Art.Rgt.	1	I	1.Kav.Div.
Reit.Art.Rgt.	1	I	XV.Kos.Kav. Korps
Afrika Art.Rgt. (mot)	1		
Art.Rgt.(mot)	2	II	2.Inf.Div.(mot)
Pz.Art.Rgt.	2	II	12.Pz.Div.
II./Art.Rgt.	2	II	H.Tr.
Afrika Art.Rgt. (mot)	2		
	3	III	3.Inf.Div.
Art.Rgt.(mot)	3	III	3.Inf.Div.(mot) 3.Pz.Gren.Div.
Res.Art.Rgt.	3	III	
	4	IV	4.Inf.Div.
(Pz.)Art.Rgt.(mot)	4	IV	14.Pz.Div.
	5	V	5.Inf.Div. 5.Jäg.Div.
	6	VI	6.Inf.Div.
	7	VII	7.Inf.Div.
	8	VIII	8.Inf.Div. 8.Jäg.Div.
	9	IX	9.Inf.Div.
	10	XIII	10.Inf.Div.
Art.Rgt.(mot)	10	XIII	10.Inf.Div.(mot) 10.Pz.Gren.Div.
	11	I	11.Inf.Div.
	12	II	12.Inf.Div.
(Pz.)Art.Rgt.(mot)	13	XI	13.Inf.Div.(mot) 13.Pz.Div.
	14	IV	14.Inf.Div.
Ldw.,Art.Abt.	14	V	
	15	IX	15.Inf.Div.
	16	VI	16.Inf.Div.
(Pz.)Art.Rgt.	16	VI	16.Pz.Div.
	17	XIII	17.Inf.Div.
	18	VIII	18.Inf.Div.
Art.Rgt.(mot)	18	VIII	18.Inf.Div.(mot) 18.Pz.Gren.Div.
schw.Art.Abt.	18		H.Tr.

Troop Unit (Artillery Regt.)		Replacement District	War Structure Subordination
Art.Kampf Btl.	18	IV	18.Art.Div.
	19	XI	19.Inf.Div.
(Pz.)Art.Rgt.	19	XI	19.Pz.Div.
Art.Rgt.(mot)	20	X	20.Inf.Div.(mot) 20.Pz.Gren.Div.
	21	I	21.Inf.Div.
	22	X	22.Inf.Div.(LL)
	23	III	23.Inf.Div.
(Pz.)Art.Rgt.	23	III	26.Pz.Div.
	24	IV	24.Inf.Div.
	25	V	25.Inf.Div.
Art.Rgt.(mot)	25	V	25.Inf.Div.(mot) 25.Pz.Gren.Div.
	26	VI	26.Inf.Div.
	27	VII	27.Inf.Div.
(Pz.)Art.Rgt.	27	VII	17.Pz.Div.
	28	VIII	28.Inf.Div. 28.Jäg.Div.
Art.Rgt.(mot)	29	IX	29.Inf.Div.(mot) 29.Pz.Gren.Div.
II./Art.Rgt.(mot)	29	IX	Pz.Vbd.Ostpr.
	30	X	30.Inf.Div.
	31	XI	31.Inf.Div.
	32	II	32.Inf.Div.
	33	XII	33.Inf.Div.
Art.Rgt.(mot)	33	XII	15.Pz.Div. 15.Pz.Gren.Div.
	34	XII	34.Inf.Div.
	35	V	35.Inf.Div.
	36	XII	36.Inf.Div.
I./Art.Rgt.	37	I	1.Inf.Div.
II.(mot)/Art.Rgt.	37	I	A.O.K.3 H.Tr.
I.(mot)/Art.Rgt.	38	II	2.Inf.Div.(mot)
II.(mot)/Art.Rgt.	38	II	II.A.K. H.Tr.
I./Art.Rgt.	39	III	3.Inf.Div.
II.(mot)/Art.Rgt.	39	III	III.A.K. H.Tr.
I./Art.Rgt.	40	IV	4.Inf.Div. 168.Inf.Div.
II.(mot)/Art.Rgt.	40	IV	IV.A.K. H.Tr.
(s.)(Pz.Haub.)Art.Abt.	40	IV	Fü.Gren.Brig.
Stab/Art.Rgt.(mot)	41	V	V.A.K. H.Tr.
I./Art.Rgt.	41	V	5.Inf.Div.
II.(mot)/Art.Rgt.	41	V	H.Tr.
I./Art.Rgt.	42	VI	6.Inf.Div.
II.(mot)/Art.Rgt.	42	VI	VI.A.K.(1939) H.Tr.
I./Art.Rgt.	43	VII	7.Inf.Div.
II.(mot)/Art.Rgt.	43	VII	VII.A.K. H.Tr.

Troop Unit (Artillery Regt.)		Replacement District	War Structure Subordination
I./Art.Rgt.	44	VIII	8.Inf.Div.
II.(mot)/Art.Rgt.	44	VIII	VIII.A.K.(1939) H.Tr.
I./Art.Rgt.	45	IX	9.Inf.Div.
II.(mot)/Art.Rgt.	45	IX	IX.A.K.(1939) XIX.A.K.(mot) H Tr.
I./Art.Rgt.	46	XIII	10.Inf.Div.
II.(mot)/Art.Rgt.	46	XIII	XIII.A.K.(1939) H.Tr.
I./Art.Rgt.	47	I	11.Inf.Div.
II.(mot)/Art.Rgt.	47	I	A.O.K.3 H.Tr.
le.Art.Abt.(mot)	47	X	I.R.47
I./Art.Rgt.	48	II	12.Inf.Div.
II.(mot)/Art.Rgt.	48	II	H.Tr.
Stab/Art.Rgt.(mot)	49	XI	XIV.A.K.(mot) XVIII.A.K. H.Tr.
I.(mot)/Art.Rgt.	49	XI	13.Inf.Div.(mo
II.(mot)/Art.Rgt.	49	XI	XIV.A.K.(mot) H.Tr.
Art.Rgt.Stab	50	III	50.Inf.Div.
I./Art.Rgt.	50	IV	14.Inf.Div.
II.(mot)/Art.Rgt.	50	IV	IV.A.K.(1939) H.Tr.
Stab/Art.Rgt.	51	IX	15.Inf.Div.
I.Art.Rgt.	51	IX	15.Inf.Div.
II.(mot)/Art.Rgt.	51	IX	IX.A.K.(1939) H.Tr.
le.Art.Abt.	53		H.Tr.
I./Art.Rgt.	52	VI	16.Inf.Div.
II.(mot)/Art.Rgt.	52	VI	H.Tr.
	53		53.Inf.Div.
I./Art.Rgt.	53	XIII	17.Inf.Div.
II.(mot)/Art.Rgt.	53	XIII	XIII.A.K.(1939) H.Tr. 15.Pz.Gren.Div.
I./Art.Rgt.	54	VIII	18.Inf.Div.
II.(mot)/Art.Rgt.	54	VII	H.Tr.
I./Art.Rgt.	55	XI	19.Inf.Div.
II.(mot)/Art.Rgt.	55	XI	XI.A.K. H.Tr.
Kos.Art.Abt.I.u.II/	55	I	1.Kos.Kav.Div./ XV.Kos.K.
I.(mot)/Art.Rgt.	56	X	20.Inf.Div.(mot)
II.(mot)/Art.Rgt.	56	X	XIV.A.K.(mot) XIX.A.K.(mot) H.Tr. 1.Pz.Div.
I./Art.Rgt.	57	I	21.Inf.Div.
II.(mot)/Art.Rgt.	57	I	A.O.K.3 H.Tr.
I./Art.Rgt.	58	X	22.Inf.Div. 197.Inf.Div.
II.(mot)/Art.Rgt.	58	X	X.A.K.(1939) H.Tr.

Troop Unit (Artillery Regt.)		Replacement District	War Structure Subordination
s.Art.Abt.	58	X	H.Tr.
I./Art.Rgt.	59	III	23.Inf.Div.
II.(mot)/Art.Rgt.	59	III	III.A.K.(1939) H.Tr.
Art.Rgt.	59(?)		1.Ski Jäg.Div.
I./Art.Rgt.	60	IV	24.Inf.Div.
II.(mot)/Art.Rgt.	60	IV	H.Tr.
I./Art.Rgt.	61	V	25.Inf.Div.
II.(mot)/Art.Rgt.	61	V	V.A.K.(1939) H.Tr.
I./Art.Rgt.	62	VI	26.Inf.Div.
II.(mot)/Art.Rgt.	62	VI	VI.A.K.(1939) H.Tr.
I./Art.Rgt.	63	VII	27.Inf.Div.
II.(mot)/Art.Rgt.	63	VII	VII.A.K.(mot) H.Tr.
I./Art.Rgt.	64	VIII	28.Inf.Div.
II.(mot)/Art.Rgt.	64	VIII	VIII.A.K.(1939) H.Tr.
I.(mot)/Art.Rgt.	65	IX	29.Inf.Div.(mot)
II.(mot)/Art.Rgt.	65	IX	H.Tr.
le.H.-Art.Abt. (mot)	65		H.Tr.
I.(mot)/Art.Rgt.	66	X	30.Inf.Div.
II.(mot)/Art.Rgt.	66	X	X.A.K.(1939) H.Tr.
I./Art.Rgt.	67	XI	31.Inf.Div.
II.(mot)/Art.Rgt.	67	XI	XI.A.K.(1939) H.Tr./56.Inf.Div.
I./Art.Rgt.	68	II	32.Inf.Div.
II.(mot)/Art.Rgt.	68	II	H.Tr.
Stab/Art.Rgt.(mot)	69	XII	XII.A.K.(1939) H.Tr.
I./Art.Rgt.	69	XII	33.Inf.Div.
II.(mot)/Art.Rgt.	69	XII	XII.A.K.(1939) H.Tr.
Stab/Art.Rgt.	70	XII	H.Tr.
I./Art.Rgt.	70	XII	34.Inf.Div.
II.(mot)/Art.Rgt.	70	XII	XII.A.K.(1939) H.Tr.
I./Art.Rgt.	71	V	35.Inf.Div.
II.(mot)/Art.Rgt.	71	V	V.A.K.(1939)
H.-Art.Abt.(mot)	71	V	H.Tr.
I./Art.Rgt.	72	XII	36.Inf.Div.
II.(mot)/Art.Rgt.	72	XII	H.Tr.
(Pz.)Art.Rgt.	73	IX	1.Pz.Div.
(Pz.)Art.Rgt.	74	XVII	2.Pz.Div.
(Pz.)Art.Rgt.	75	III	3.Pz.Div.

Troop Unit (Artillery Regt.)	Replacement District	War Structure Subordination
I./Art. Rgt. (mot) 75	III	5. le. Afr. Div.
(Pz.)Art. Rgt. (mot) 76	VI	1. le. Div.
		6. Pz. Div.
I. (mot)/Art. Rgt. 77	V	H. Tr.
		V. A. K. (1939)
II. (mot)/Art. Rgt. 77	V	H. Tr.
(Pz.)Art. Rgt. (mot) 78	IX	2. le. Div.
		7. Pz. Div.
Geb. Art. Rgt. 79	VII	1. Geb. Div.
(Pz.)Art. Rgt. (mot) 80	III	3. le. Div.
		8. Pz. Div.
81	VII	97. le. Div.
		97. Jäg. Div.
(Geb.)Art. Rgt. 82	XIII	99. le. Div.
		99. Jäg. Div.
II./Geb. Art. Rgt. 82	XIII	9. Geb. Div.
83	XVII	100. le. Div.
		100. Jäg. Div.
I. (mot)/Art. Rgt. 84	IV	H. Tr.
II. (mot)/Art. Rgt. 84	IV	H. Tr.
85	V	101. le. Div.
		101. Jäg. Div.
86	XII	112. Inf. Div.
87	XIII	113. Inf. Div.
(Pz.)Art. Rgt. (mot) 88	IV	18. Pz. Div.
		18. Art. Div.
(Pz.)Art. Rgt. (mot) 89	I	24. Pz. Div.
(Pz.)Art. Rgt. (mot) 90	V	10. Pz. Div.
Pz. Art. Rgt. 91	VI	25. Pz. Div.
H. -Art. Abt. (mot) 91		H. Tr.
(Pz.)Art. Rgt. (mot) 92	IX	20. Pz. Div.
II. (mot)/Art. Rgt. 93	XIII	H. Tr.
		4. Pz. Div.
Pz. Art. Rgt. 93	III	26. Pz. Div.
Geb. Art. Rgt. 94	VII	4. Geb. Div.
Geb. Art. Rgt. 95	XVIII	5. Geb. Div.
96	XVII	44. Inf. Div.
I./Art. Rgt. 97	XVII	44. Inf. Div.
98	XVII	45. Inf. Div.
I./Art. Rgt. 99	XVII	45. Inf. Div.
schw. H. -Art. Abt. (mot) 99		H. Tr./7. Geb. Div.
Eisb. Art. Lehr-u. Ers. Abt. 100	II	Ch H Rüst u. BdE
Grz. Art. Abt. (mot) 101	III	Grz. Sch. Abschn. Kdo. 12
Art. Lehr Abt. 101		271. Inf. Div.
(Pz.)Art. Rgt. (mot) 102	XVII	4. le. Div.
		9. Pz. Div.
Grz. Art. Abt. (mot) 102	III	Grz. Sch. Abschn. Kdo. 12

Troop Unit (Artillery Regt.)	Replacement District	War Structure Subordination
(Pz.)Art. Rgt. (mot) 103	XIII	4. Pz. Div.
Grz. Art. Abt. (mot) 103	III	Grz. Sch. Abschn. Kdo. 12
104	VIII	102. Inf. Div.
I. (mot)/Grz. Art. Rgt. 105	XII	Gen. Kdo. Grz. Tr. Saarpfalz
I. (mot)/Art. Rgt. 105	XII	H. Tr.
le. H. -Art. Abt. (mot) 105	XII	H. Tr.
I. (mot)/Grz. Art. Rgt. 106	XII	Gen. Kdo. Grz. Tr. Saarpfalz
I. (mot)/Art. Rgt. 106	XII	H. Tr.
schw. H. -Art. Abt. (mot) 106	XII	H. Tr.
107	VI	106. Inf. Div.
I. (mot)/Grz. Art. Rgt. 108	XII	Gen. Kdo. Grz. Tr. Saarpfalz
I. (mot)/Grz. Art. Rgt. 109	XII	Gen. Kdo. Grz. Tr. Saarpfalz
Stab/Art. Rgt. (mot) 109	XVII	XVII. A. K. (1939) H. Tr.
I. (mot)/Art. Rgt. 109	XVII	XVII. A. K. (1939) H. Tr.
II. (mot)/Art. Rgt. 109	XVII	XVII. A. K. (1939) H. Tr
III. (mot)/Art. Rgt. 109	XVII	XVIII. A. K. (1939) H. Tr.
IV. (mot)/Art. Rgt. 109		H. Tr.
Stab/Art. Rgt. (mot) 110	XVIII	H. Tr.
I. (mot)/Art. Rgt. 110	XVII	2. Pz. Div.
Geb. Art. Rgt. 111	XVIII	2. Geb. Div.
III. (mot)/Geb. Art. Rgt. 111	XVIII	2. Geb. Div. H. Tr.
Geb. Art. Rgt. 112	XVIII	3. Geb. Div.
I./Geb. Art. Rgt. 112	XVIII	9. Geb. Div.
III. (mot)/Geb. Art. Rgt. 112	XVIII	2. Geb. Div. 6. Geb. Div. (1941) H. Tr. (1940)
I./Geb. Art. Rgt. 113	XVIII	2. Geb. Div.
114	XIII	46. Inf. Div.
Stab/Art. Rgt. 115	XIII	46. Inf. Div.
I./Art. Rgt. 115	XIII	46. Inf. Div.
II. (mot)/Art. Rgt. 115	XIII	H. Tr.
(Pz.)Art. Rgt. (mot) 116	VIII	5. Pz. Div.
117	XI	111. Inf. Div.
Geb. Art. Abt. 118	XII	A. O. K. 1
Geb. Art. Rgt. 118	XVIII	6. Geb. Div.

Troop Unit (Artillery Regt.)	Replacement District	War Structure Subordination
(Pz.)Art.Rgt.(mot) 119	VIII	11.Pz.Div.
119	XI	19.V.G.Div.
120	X	110.Inf.Div.
121	I	121.Inf.Div.
122	II	122.Inf.Div.
123	III	123.Inf.Div.
Geb.Art.Abt. 124	XVIII	139.Geb.Jäg.Brig.
		9.Geb.Div.(1945)
Geb.Art.Rgt. 124	XVIII	8.Geb.Div.
125	V	125.Inf.Div.
125	VI	126.Inf.Div.
Pz.Art.Rgt. 127		27.Pz.Div.
Pz.Art.Rgt. 128	V	23.Pz.Div.
129	IX	129.Inf.Div.
Pz.Art.Rgt. 130	III	Pz.Lehr Div.
131	XI	131.Inf.Div.
132	XII	132.Inf.Div.
Art.Rgt.(mot) 133		H.Tr.
134	IV	134.Inf.Div.
Art.Rgt. 135		H.Tr.
137	XVII	137.Inf.Div.
138	III	38.Inf.Div.
139	VI	39.Inf.Div.
Art.Rgt.(mot) 140	XII	22.Pz.Div.
141		41.Fest.Div.
142	XVII	42.Jäg.Div.
(Pz.)Art.Rgt.(mot) 146	VI	16.Inf.Div.(mot)
		16.Pz.Gren.Div.
		116.Pz.Div.
147	VI	47.Inf.Div.
148	XI	48.Inf.Div.
149	XI	49.Inf.Div.
150	III	50.Inf.Div.
schw.Art.Abt. 151	I	Fest.Tr.
schw.H.-Art.Abt.(mot) 151	I	H.Tr.
schw.Bttr. 152		H.Tr.
152	IX	52.Inf.Div.
schw.Art.Abt.(mot) 153	III	H.Tr.
153		53.Inf.Div.
schw.Art.Abt.(mot) 154	VIII	H.Tr.
Art.Abt. 155		155.Feldhaub.Div.
(Pz.)Art.Rgt.(mot) 155	III	21.Pz.Div.
156	IV	56.Inf.Div.
157	VII	57.Inf.Div.
158	X	58.Inf.Div.
159	II	59.Inf.Div.
160	XX	60.Inf.Div.
Art.Rgt.(mot) 160	XX	60.Inf.Div.(mot)
Ldw.Art.Rgt. 161	I	Fest.Tr.Lötzen
		301.Inf.Div.
161	I	61.Inf.Div.
162	VIII	62.Inf.Div.
164	VI	64.Inf.Div.
165	XII	65.Inf.Div.
168	III	68.Inf.Div.
169	VI	69.Inf.Div.
170	V	70.Inf.Div.
171	XI	71.Inf.Div.
172	VI	72.Inf.Div.
173	XIII	73.Inf.Div.
Art.Abt. 174		H.Tr.
175	II	75.Inf.Div.
176	III	76.Inf.Div.
177	V	77.Inf.Div.
178	V	78.Inf.Div.
		78.Sturm Div. tmot.
Feldausb.Art.Abt. 178		H.Tr.
179	VIII	79.Inf.Div.
180	X	180.Inf.Div.
181	VIII	81.Inf.Div.
182	IX	82.Inf.Div.
183	X	83.Inf.Div.
184	VI	84.Inf.Div.
III.(mot)/Art.Rgt. 184	VI	H.Tr.
185	XII	85.Inf.Div.
186	VI	86.Inf.Div.
187	IV	87.Inf.Div.
188	XIII	88.Inf.Div.
189	X	89.Inf.Div.
Art.Rgt.(mot) 190	III	90.le.Afr.Div.
		90.Pz.Gren.Div.
Art.Rgt.(tmot) 191	XII	91.Inf.Div.
Art.Abt. 191	XI	191.Inf.Div.
192	XVII	92.Inf.Div.
le.Art.Abt.(mot) 192	II	92.Gren.Brig.(mot)
193	III	93.Inf.Div.
194	IV	94.Inf.Div.
195	IX	95.Inf.Div.
196	XI	96.Inf.Div.
schw.Art.Abt.(mot) 196	V	H.Tr.
198	XIII	98.Inf.Div.
199	VI	199.Inf.Div.
Art.Rgt.(Stab?) 200		H.Tr.
Art.Abt. 201	IX	201.Sich.Brig.
Art.Abt. 202		202.Sich.Brig.
Art.Abt.(Rgt.) 203	III	203.Sich.Brig.
		203.Sich.Div.
Art.Abt. 204		204.Sich.Brig.
205	V	205.Inf.Div.
206	I	206.Inf.Div.
207	II	207.Inf.Div.
I./Art.Rgt. 207	II	207.Sich.Div.
II./Art.Rgt. 207	II	281.Sich.Div.
III./Art.Rgt. 207	VIII	285.Sich.Div.
IV./Art.Rgt. 207	II	H.Tr.
208	III	208.Inf.Div.
209	IV	209.Inf.Div.
II.u.III./Art.Rgt. 209	IV	H.Tr.
IV.(mot)/Art.Rgt. 209	IV	H.Tr.
210		210.Inf.Div.
211	VI	211.Inf.Div.

Troop Unit (Artillery Regt.)	Replacement District	War Structure Subordination
	212 VII	212.Inf.Div.
Art.Rgt.(Abt.)	213 VIII	213.Inf.Div.
I./Art.Rgt.	213 VIII	213.Sich.Div.
		320.Inf.Div.
II./Art.Rgt.	213 VIII	286.Inf.Div.
III./Art.Rgt.	213 III	403.Sich.Div.
		201.Sich.Div.
	214 IX	214.Inf.Div.
	215 V	215.Inf.Div.
	216 XI	216.Inf.Div.
	217 I	217.Inf.Div.
	218 III	218.Inf.Div.
IV.(mot)/Art.Rgt.	218 III	H.Tr.
	219 XIII	183.Inf.Div.
	220 IV	164.Inf.Div.
		164.le.Afr.Div.
Art.Abt.(Rgt.)	221 VIII	221.Inf.Div.
I./Art.Rgt.	221 VIII	221.Sich.Div.
II./Art.Rgt.	221 VIII	444.Sich.Div.
III./Art.Rgt.	221 VIII	454.Sich.Div.
	222 XI	181.Inf.Div.
	223 IV	223.Inf.Div.
I.u.III./Art.Rgt.	223 IV	H.Tr.
IV.(mot)/Art.Rgt.	223 IV	H.Tr.
	225 X	225.Inf.Div.
	226 VIII	226.Inf.Div.
	227 VI	227.Inf.Div.
Art.Abt.	228 I	228.Inf.Div.
	229 XXI	197.Inf.Div.
	230 IX	169.Inf.Div.
Art.Abt.	231 XIII	231.Inf.Div.
I./Art.Rgt.	231 XIII	H.Tr.
II./Art.Rgt.	231 XIII	H.Tr.
		6.Geb.Div.
III./Art.Rgt.	231 XIII	H.Tr.
IV.(mot)/Art.Rgt.	231 XIII	H.Tr.
	232 IX	232.Inf.Div.
	233 XX	196.Inf.Div.
	234 III	163.Inf.Div.
IV.(mot)/Art.Rgt.	234 III	H.Tr.
	235 V	198.Inf.Div.
	236 II	162.Inf.Div.
	237 XIII	237.Inf.Div.
	238 VII	167.Inf.Div.
Art.Abt.(Rgt.)	239 VIII	239.Inf.Div.
IV.(mot)/Art.Rgt.	239 VIII	H.Tr.
	240 X	170.Inf.Div.
	241 I	161.Inf.Div.
	242 II	242.Inf.Div.
	243 XVII	243.Inf.Div.
	244 I	244.Inf.Div.
	245 V	245.Inf.Div.
	246 XII	246.Inf.Div.
schw.Art.Abt.	247	H.Tr.
	248 VIII	168.Inf.Div.
	250 XIII	250.Inf.Div.
	251 IX	251.Inf.Div.
IV.(mot)/Art.Rgt.	251 IX	H.Tr.
	252 VIII	252.Inf.Div.

Troop Unit (Artillery Regt.)	Replacement District	War Structure Subordination
	253 VI	253.Inf.Div.
IV.(mot)/Art.Rgt.	253 VI	H.Tr.
	254 VI	254.Inf.Div.
	255 IV	255.Inf.Div.
IV.(mot)/Art.Rgt.	255 IV	H.Tr.
	256 IV	256.Inf.Div.
IV.(mot)/Art.Rgt.	256 IV	H.Tr.
	257 III	257.Inf.Div.
	258 II	258.Inf.Div.
IV.(mot)/Art.Rgt.	258 II	H.Tr.
	260 V	260.Inf.Div.
schw.H.-Art.Abt.	260 V	H.Tr.
	262 XVII	262.Inf.Div.
	263 XII	263.Inf.Div.
IV.(mot)Art.Rgt.	263 XII	H.Tr.
	264 VI	264.Inf.Div.
	265 XI	265.Inf.Div.
	266 V	266.Inf.Div.
	267 XI	267.Inf.Div.
IV.(mot)/Art.Rgt.	267 XI	H.Tr.
	268 VII	268.Inf.Div.
IV.(mot)/Art.Rgt.	268 VII	H.Tr.
	269 X	269.Inf.Div.
IV.(mot)/Art.Rgt.	269 X	H.Tr.
		69.Inf.Div.
Art.Abt.	270 X	270.Küst.Vert.Div.
	271 XIII	271.Inf.Div.
	272 XI	272.Inf.Div.
Res.Art.Abt.	273	H.Tr.
schw.H.-Art.Abt. (mot)	273	H.Tr.
	274 II	274.Inf.Div.
	275 IV	275.Inf.Div.
	276 XI	276.Inf.Div
	277 XVII	277.Inf.Div.
	278 III	278.Inf.Div.
Art.Abt.	281 II	281.Sich.Div.
	282 V	282.Inf.Div.
Art.Abt.	285 II	285.Sich.Div.
Art.Abt.(mot)	287	Sd.Vbd.287
Art.Abt.(mot)	288	Sd.Vbd.288
	288	288.Inf.Div.
H.-Art.Rgt.(mot)	288	18.Art.Div.
	290 X	290.Inf.Div.
	291 I	291.Inf.Div.
	292 II	292.Inf.Div.
	293 III	293.Inf.Div.
	294 IV	294.Inf.Div.
	295 XI	295.Inf.Div.
	296 XIII	296.Inf.Div.
	297 XVII	297.Inf.Div.
	298 VIII	298.Inf.Div.
	299 IX	299.Inf.Div.
	300 III	Pol.Div.
Abt.	300	H.Tr.
I./Art.Rgt.	301 I	301.Inf.Div.

Troop Unit (Artillery Regt.)		Replacement District	War Structure Subordination
	302	II	302. Inf. Div.
	303	III	303. Inf. Div.
	304	IV	304. Inf. Div.
	305	V	305. Inf. Div.
	306	VI	306. Inf. Div.
	309	III	309. Inf. Div.
	310	X	310. Inf. Div.
I./Art. Rgt.	311	I	311. Inf. Div.
	317	XVII	317. Inf. Div.
	319	IX	319. Inf. Div.
	320	VIII	320. Inf. Div.
	321	XI	321. Inf. Div.
	323	XII	323. Inf. Div.
	326	VI	326. Inf. Div.
	327	XVII	327. Inf. Div.
	328	II	328. Inf. Div.
	329	VI	329. Inf. Div.
	330	V	330. Inf. Div.
	331	XVII	331. Inf. Div.
	332	VIII	332. Inf. Div.
	333	III	333. Inf. Div.
	334	XIII	334. Inf. Div.
	335	V	335. Inf. Div.
	336	IV	336. Inf. Div.
	337	VII	337. Inf. Div.
	338	II	338. Inf. Div.
	339	IX	339. Inf. Div.
	340	XX	340. Inf. Div.
	341		341. Inf. Div.
	342	XII	342. Inf. Div.
	343	XIII	343. Inf. Div.
	344		344. Inf. Div.
IV. (mot)/Art. Rgt.	344	V	H. Tr.
Art. Abt. (mot)	345		345. Pz. Gren. Div.
	346	IX	346. Inf. Div.
schw. H. -Art. Abt.	346		H. Tr.
	347	XI	347. Inf. Div.
	348	XII	348. Inf. Div.
	349	I	349. Inf. Div.
	351	XVII	351. Inf. Div.
	352	XI	352. Inf. Div.
	353	II	353. Inf. Div.
	355	V	355. Inf. Div.
	356	IX	356. Inf. Div.
	357	IV	357. Inf. Div.
	358	VIII	358. Inf. Div.
	359	III	359. Inf. Div.
le. Afr. Art. Abt.	361		Afr. Schtz. Rgt. 361
	361	VI	361. Inf. Div.
	362	VII	362. Inf. Div.
	363	IX	363. Inf. Div.
	364	V	364. Inf. Div.
	365	V	365. Inf. Div.
	367	VII	367. Inf. Div.
	369	XVII	369. Inf. Div.
	370	VIII	370. Inf. Div.
	371	VI	371. Inf. Div.
	372	IV	372. Inf. Div.
	373	XVII	373. Inf. Div.
schw. Art. Abt.	373		H. Tr.
	376	VII	376. Inf. Div.
	377	IX	377. Inf. Div.

Troop Unit (Artillery Regt.)		Replacement District	War Structure Subordination
	379	IX	379. Inf. Div.
	380	III	380. Inf. Div.
	383	III	383. Inf. Div.
	384	IV	384. Inf. Div.
	385	VI	385. Inf. Div.
	386	VI	386. Inf. Div.
Art. Abt. (mot)	386		
	387	VII	387. Inf. Div.
	389	XII	389. Inf. Div.
	392	XVII	392. Inf. Div.
	393	X	393. Inf. Div.
	395	I	395. Inf. Div.
	399	I	399. Inf. Div.
gem. Art. Abt. (mot)	400	III	Inf. Rgt. (mot) GD
schw. Art. Abt.	400	IV	H. Tr.
Stab/Art. Rgt.	401	I	H. Tr.
Stab/Art. Rgt.	402		H. Tr.
Art. Rgt. (mot)	404	X	H. Tr.
schw. Art. Abt. (mot)	405		H. Tr.
schw. Art. Abt.	406		H. Tr.
schw. Art. Abt. (mot)	408		H. Tr.
schw. Art. Abt. (mot)	412		H. Tr.
schw. Art. Abt.	415		H. Tr.
Art. Abt. (Rgt.)	416	X	416. Inf. Div.
schw. Art. Abt.	420		H. Tr.
schw. Art. Abt. (mot)	422	X	H. Tr.
le. Art. Abt. (mot)	423	XI	H. Tr./1. Ski Jg. Div.
Art. Abt. (mot)	424		H. Tr.
le. Art. Abt. (mot)	424		7. Geb. Div.
schw. Bttr.	425		H. Tr.
le. Art. Abt. (mot)	426	II	H. Tr.
schw. Art. Abt. (mot)	427	VII	
			H. Tr.
schw. Bttr.	428		H. Tr.
le. Art. Abt. (mot)	429		H. Tr.
schw. Art. Abt. (mot)	430	VII	
			H. Tr.
le. Art. Abt. (mot)	430	XI	H. Tr.
schw. Art. Abt. (mot)	435		H. Tr.
Stab/Art. Rgt. z. b. V. 435 (mot)			H. Tr.
schw. Art. Abt. (mot)	436	II	II. A. K. (1939)
			H. Tr.
Stab/Art. Rgt. z. b. V. 436			H. Tr.
le. Art. Abt. (mot)	436		H. Tr.
le. H. -Art. Abt.	440		H. Tr.
	440		440. Inf. Div.
s. F. H. Zug(Sf.)(bod)	441		LXXXVIII. A. K.
s. F. H. Zug(Sf.)(bod)	442		
schw. Art. Abt. (mot)	442		H. Tr.
schw. Art. Abt.	443		H. Tr.
Fernraketen Lehr- u. Versuchs Bttr.	444	II	H. Tr.
schw. Art. Abt. (mot)	445	X	
			H. Tr.
schw. Art. Abt. (mot)	446	XI	
			H. Tr.
schw. Art. Abt. (mot)	447		H. Tr.
schw. Art. Abt. (mot)	450	V	H. Tr.
schw. Art. Abt.	451	XII	H. Tr.

Troop Unit (Artillery Regt.)	Replacement District	War Structure Subordination
schw. Art. Abt. 452		H. Tr.
schw. Art. Abt. 454		H. Tr.
schw. Art. Abt. (mot) 456	VIII	H. Tr.
schw. Art. Abt. (mot) 457	X	H. Tr.
schw. Art. Abt. (mot) 458	VII	H. Tr.
Eisb. Bttr. 459		H. Tr.
schw. Art. Abt. (mot) 460	VIII	H. Tr.
schw. Art. Abt. (mot) 464		H. Tr.
schw. Bttr. 1. u. 2. / 477		H. Tr.
Art. Abt. (mot) 482		H. Tr.
Art. Abt. (mot) 485		H. Tr.
Stab/Art. Rgt. z.b.V. 485 (mot)		H. Tr.
schw. Art. Abt. (mot) 488		H. Tr.
schw. Art. Abt. (mot) 489		H. Tr.
schw. Art. Abt. (mot) 490		H. Tr.
schw. Art. Abt. (mot) 491		H. Tr.
schw. Art. Abt. (mot) 492		H. Tr.
schw. Bttr. 493		H. Tr.
schw. Art. Abt. (mot) 496	XI	H. Tr.
schw. Art. Abt. (mot) 497		H. Tr.
Stab/Art. Rgt. z.b.V. 501 (mot)	I	AOK 3 / H. Tr.
schw. Art. Abt. 504		Div. Rossi
schw. Bttr. 505	V	H. Tr.
schw. Art. Abt. (mot) 506	I	AOK 3 / H. Tr.
schw. Art. Abt. 507		H. Tr. / 203. Sich. Div.
schw. Art. Abt. 508	I	H. Tr.
schw. Art. Abt. 509		H. Tr.
schw. Art. Abt. 510	XIII	Westbefest. Mosel/Rhein (1939/40)
Stab/Art. Rgt. z.b.V. 511 (mot)	I	A.O.K. 3 / H. Tr.
schw. Art. Abt. (mot) 511	I	A.O.K. 3 / H. Tr.
Stab/schw. Art. Abt. 517 (mot)		H. Tr.
Stab/Art. Rgt. z.b.V. 520 (mot)		H. Tr.
Art. Abt. (mot) 520		H. Tr.
Stab/Art. Abt. z.b.V. 520		H. Tr.
schw. Art. Abt. (mot) 525		H. Tr.
schw. Art. Abt. (mot) 526	I	H. Tr.
Stab/Art. Rgt. z.b.V. 526		H. Tr.
I. (mot)/Art. Rgt. 526		H. Tr.
schw. Art. Abt. (mot) 528		H. Tr.
schw. Art. Abt. 530		H. Tr.
schw. Bttr. (tmot) 531	III	H. Tr.
Eisb. Bttr. 532		H. Tr.
schw. Art. Abt. (mot) 536	I	A.O.K. 3 / H. Tr.
schw. Art. Abt. 539		
H.-Art. Stab z.b.V. 551 (mot)		H. Tr.
H.-Art. Stab z.b.V. 553 (mot)		H. Tr.

Troop Unit (Artillery Regt.)	Replacement District	War Structure Subordination
Art. Rgt. (bod.) 554	V	554. Stell. Div.
H.-Art. Stab z.b.V. 554 (mot)		H. Tr.
Art. Rgt. (bod.) 555	versch.	555. Stell. Div.
schw. Art. Abt. 555		H. Tr.
Art. Rgt. (bod.) 556	versch.	556. Stell. Div.
Art. Rgt. (bod.) 557	versch.	557. Stell. Div.
schw. Art. Abt. (mot) 557	XVIII	H. Tr. Afrika
le. Art. Abt. (mot) 558	I	H. Tr.
Stab/Art. Rgt. z.b.V. 560 (mot)	XVIII	H. Tr.
schw. Art. Abt. 560	XVIII	H. Tr.
schw. Art. Abt. 561		H. Tr.
schw. Art. Abt. 580		H. Tr.
Bttr. (Ost) 582		Ost Rgt. Stb. z.b.V. 709
Eisb. Bttr. 592		H. Tr.
schw. Art. Abt. 594		
Stab/Art. Rgt. z.b.V. 600		H. Tr.
schw. Art. Abt. (mot) 601	II	H. Tr.
schw. Art. Abt. (mot) 602		H. Tr.
Stab/Art. Rgt. z.b.V. 603		H. Tr.
le. Art. Abt. (mot) 603	XVIII	H. Tr.
schw. Art. Abt. (mot) 604	XVII II	H. Tr.
schw. Art. Abt. (mot) 605	IV	H. Tr.
Stab/Art. Rgt. z.b.V. 606 (mot)		H. Tr.
schw. Art. Abt. (mot) 606		H. Tr.
schw. Art. Abt. (mot) 607	IV	H. Tr.
schw. Bttr. 607	IV	H. Tr.
Stab/Art. Rgt. z.b.V. 608 (mot)		H. Tr.
Stab/Art. Rgt. z.b.V. 609 (mot)		
Stab/Art. Rgt. z.b.V. 610 (mot)		H. Tr.
schw. Art. Abt. (mot) 611	XIII	H. Tr.
Stab/Art. Rgt. z.b.V. 612 (mot)		H. Tr.
Stab/Art. Rgt. z.b.V. 613 (mot)		H. Tr.
Art. Abt. 613		H. Tr.
Stab/Art. Rgt. z.b.V. 614 (mot)		H. Tr.
Bttr. (Ost) 2./614		
schw. Art. Abt. (mot) 615	V	H. Tr.
schw. Art. Abt. (mot) 616	VI	H. Tr.
schw. Mrs. Bttr. (mot) 616	VI	H. Tr.
Stab/Art. Rgt. z.b.V. 617 (mot)		H. Tr.

Einheit	Nr.		
I./Art.Rgt. (mot)	617		H.Tr./1.Kav.Brig.
Stab/Art.Rgt.z.b.V.618 (mot)			H.Tr.
Stab/Art.Rgt.z.b.V. 619 (mot)			H.Tr.
Art.Rgt. (tmot)	619	XVIII	Fest.Brig.Kreta
schw.Art.Rgt.(mot)	619	XVIII	H.Tr.
schw.Art.Abt.	620	XIII	H.Tr.
Stabsbttr.f.Eisb. Art.	620	III	H.Tr.
H.-Art.Stab z.b.V. 621 (mot)		VI	H.Tr.
schw.Art.Abt.(mot)	621	VI	H.Tr.
Art.Abt.(tmot) (Ost)	621		H.Tr.
Stab/Art.Rgt.z.b.V. 622 (mot)		XI	H.Tr.
Stab/Art.Rgt.z.b.V. 623 (mot)			H.Tr.
schw.Art.Abt.(mot)	624	VIII	H.Tr.
schw.Art.Abt.(mot)	625	XI	H.Tr.
schw.Art.Abt.(mot)	626	V	H.Tr.
Stab/Art.Rgt.z.b.V.627 (mot)			H.Tr.
schw.Bttr.(mot)	628	III	H.Tr.
schw.Art.Abt.(mot)	628	III	H.Tr.
schw.Art.Abt.(mot)	629	IV	H.Tr.
schw.Art.Abt.(mot)	630	IV	H.Tr.
schw.Art.Abt.(mot)	631	VIII	H.Tr.
le.Art.Abt.(mot)	631	VIII	H.Tr.
schw.Art.Abt.(mot) (tmot)	633	IX	H.Tr.
sçhw.Art.Abt.(mot)	634	X	H.Tr.
schw.Art.Abt.(mot)	635	XII	H.Tr.
schw.Art.Abt.(mot)	636	XII	H.Tr.
schw.Art.Abt.(mot)	637	II	H.Tr.
schw.Art.Abt.(mot)	638		H.Tr.
schw.Art.Abt.(mot)	639		H.Tr.
Eisb.Bttr.	640		H.Tr.
schw.Art.Abt.(mot)	641	IV	H.Tr.
schw.Art.Abt.(mot)	642		H.Tr.
schw.Art.Abt.(mot)	643	IX	H.Tr..
schw.Art.Abt.(mot)	644	IX	H.Tr.
schw.Art.Abt.(mot)	645	III	H.Tr.
schw.Art.Abt.(mot)	646	V	H.Tr.
Stab/Eisb.Art.Rgt.	646		H.Tr.
schw.Art.Abt.(mot)	647	XII	H.Tr.
schw.Art.Abt.(mot)	648	XII	H.Tr.
schw.Art.Abt.(mot)	649	XIII	H.Tr.
Eisb.Bttr.	649		Art.Abt.720
I./Art.Rgt.	650	X	710.Inf.Div.
Art.Abt.(Rgt.)	651	XI	711.Inf.Div.
Art.Abt.(Rgt.)	652	XII	712.Inf.Div.
Art.Abt.	653	XIII	713.Inf.Div.
Art.Rgt.	653	XIII	133.Fest.Div.
Art.(Abt.) Rgt.	654	IV	704.Inf.Div. 104.Jäg.Div.
Eisb.Bttr.	655		H.Tr.
Art.(Abt.)Rgt.	656	VI	716.Inf.Div.
I./Art.Rgt.	657	VII	707.Inf.Div.
Art.(Abt.)Rgt.	658	VIII	708.Inf.Div.
schw.Art.Abt.	658		H.Tr.
schw.Art.Abt.	659		H.Tr.
schw.Art.Abt.(Eisb.)	660		H.Tr.
Art.(Abt.)Rgt.	661	B.-M.	714.Inf.Div. 114.Jäg.Div.
I./Art.Rgt.	662	II	702.Inf.Div.
Art.(Abt.)Rgt.	663	III	719.Inf.Div.
Eisb.Bttr.	664	XIII	H.Tr.
Eisb.Bttr.	665		H.Tr.
schw.Art.Abt.	666		H.Tr.
Art.(Abt.)Rgt.	668	XVIII	718.Inf.Div. 118.Jäg.Div.
Art.(Abt.)Rgt.	669	IX	709.Inf.Div.
Art.(Abt.)Rgt.	670	XVII	717.Inf.Div. 117.Jäg.Div.
Art.(Abt.)Rgt.	671	V	715.Inf.Div.
H.-Art.Rgt.	671		H.Tr.
schw.Art.Abt.	672		H.Tr.
Eisb.Bttr.	672		H.Tr.
Eisb.Bttr.	673		H.Tr.
Eisb.Bttr.	674		H.Tr.

Troop Unit (Artillery Regt.)		Replacement District	War Structure Subordination
schw. Art. Abt.	674		H. Tr.
Stab/schw. Art. Abt. z. b. V. (mot)	676	IV	H. Tr.
Stab/Eisb. Art. Rgt.	676	IV	H. Tr.
Stab/Art. Rgt. z. b. V. (mot)	677	IV	H. Tr.
Art. Rgt. (mot)	677	IV	H. Tr.
Stab/Eisb. Art. Rgt. z. b. V.	679		H. Tr.
H. -Art. Stab z. b. V. (mot)	679		H. Tr.
schw. Art. Abt. (mot)	680	IX	H. Tr.
Eisb. Art. Abt. Stab z. b. V.	680		H. Tr.
Stab/Eisb. Art. Rgt. z. b. V.	681		H. Tr.
H. -Art. Stab z. b. V. (mot)	681	IX	H. Tr.
schw. Art. Abt. (mot)	681	IX	H. Tr.
Art. Rgt. (mot)	684		H. Tr.
Eisb. Bttr.	685		H. Tr.
Eisb. Bttr.	686		H. Tr.
Eisb. Bttr.	687		H. Tr.
Eisb. Bttr.	688		H. Tr.
Eisb. Bttr.	689		H. Tr.
Eisb. Bttr.	690		H. Tr.
Eisb. Bttr.	691	III	H. Tr.
Eisb. Bttr.	692		H. Tr.
Eisb. Bttr.	693		H. Tr.
Eisb. Bttr.	694		H. Tr.
Eisb. Bttr.	695		H. Tr.
Eisb. Bttr.	696		H. Tr.
Art. Rgt. (mot)	697		H. Tr.
H. -Art. Stab z.b.V. (mot)	697		H. Tr.
schw. Bttr. (mot)	698		H. Tr.
Eisb. Bttr.	698		H. Tr.
II. /Art. Rgt.	699		H. Tr.
Eisb. Bttr.	701		H. Tr.
Stab/Eisb. Art. Rgt. z. b. V.	702	IV	H. Tr.
Stab/Art. Rgt. z. b. V. (mot)	704		H. Tr.
Eisb. Art. Abt. Stab z. b. V.	704		H. Tr.
Eisb. Bttr.	704		H. Tr.

Troop Unit (Artillery Regt.)		Replacement District	War Structure Subordination
Stab/Art. Rgt.	705		H. Tr.
schw. Art. Abt. (mot)	705	XII	H. Tr.
schw. Art. Abt. (mot)	707		H. Tr.
schw. Art. Abt.	708	X	H. Tr.
Stab/Art. Rgt.	708		H. Tr.
schw. Art. Abt. (mot)	709	III	H. Tr.
Art. Rgt.	709	IX	709. Inf. Div.
Eisb. Bttr.	710		H. Tr.
Eisb. Bttr.	711		H. Tr.
schw. Art. Abt. (mot)	712	IV	H. Tr.
Eisb. Bttr.	712		H. Tr.
Eisb. Bttr.	713		H. Tr.
schw. Art. Abt. (mot)	714	V	H. Tr.
le. Art. Abt. (mot)	714	V	H. Tr. / 3. Pz. Div.
Eisb. Bttr.	715		H. Tr.
schw. Art. Abt. (mot)	716	IX	H. Tr.
Eisb. Bttr.	717		H. Tr.
Eisb. Bttr.	718		H. Tr.
Eisb. Bttr.	719	VI	H. Tr.
Art. Rgt.	719		719. Inf. Div.
Stab/Eisb. Art. Rgt. z. b. V.	720		H. Tr.
Eisb. Bttr.	721		H. Tr.
Eisb. Bttr.	722		H. Tr.
Stab/Eisb. Art. Abt. z. b. V.	725		H. Tr.
Eisb. Bttr.	725	VIII	H. Tr.
Eisb. Bttr.	726		H. Tr.
Stab/Eisb. Art. Rgt. z. b. V.	726		H. Tr.
H. -Art. Stab z. b. V. (mot)	726		H. Tr.
Art. Abt.	729		H. Tr.
Eisb. Bttr.	729		H. Tr.
Art. Abt.	730	VI	H. Tr. (2. Geb. Div.)
schw. Art. Abt. (mot)	731	VIII	H. Tr.
schw. Art. Abt. (mot)	732	X	H. Tr.
schw. Art. Abt. (mot)	733	XII	H. Tr.
schw. Art. Abt. (mot)	735	IX	H. Tr.
schw. Art. Abt. (mot)	736	XIII	H, Tr.
schw. Art. Abt. (mot)	737	XVII	H. Tr.

Troop Unit (Artillery Regt.)		Replacement District	War Structure Subordination	Troop Unit (Artillery Regt.)		Replacement District	War Structure Subordination
schw. Art. Abt. (mot)	740		H. Tr.	Stab/Art. Rgt. z.b. V. (mot)	782		H. Tr.
							18. Art. Div.
			18. Art. Div.	Stab/Art. Rgt. z.b. V. (mot)	783		H. Tr.
le. Art. Abt. (mot)	741	II	H. Tr.	schw. Bttr. (mot)	784		H. Tr.
schw. Art. Abt.	743		H. Tr.	Stab/Art. Rgt. z.b. V. (mot)	785	X	H. Tr.
Eisb. Bttr.	744		H. Tr.	Stab/Art. Rgt. z.b. V. (mot)	786		H. Tr.
le. Art. Abt.	745	VI	H. Tr.				
le. Art. Abt. (mot)	747		H. Tr.	schw. Art. Abt. z.b. V. (mot)	786		H. Tr.
le. Art. Abt. (mot)	749	XI	H. Tr.	Stab/Art. Rgt. z.b. V. (mot)	787		H. Tr.
Eisb. Bttr.	749		H. Tr.	Stab/Art. Rgt. z.b. V. (mot)	788		H. Tr.
le. Art. Abt. (mot)	751	XII	H. Tr.	Stab/Art. Rgt. z.b. V. (mot)	792	II	H. Tr.
Eisb. Bttr.	752		H. Tr.	schw. Art. Abt.	793		H. Tr.
Art. Abt. (Ost)	752		H. Tr.	Stab/Art. Rgt. z.b. V. (mot)	797		H. Tr.
le. Art. Abt.	753	IV	H. Tr.				
schw. Art. Abt.	754		H. Tr.	Stab/Art. Abt. z.b. V. (mot)	800	IV	H. Tr.
le. Art. Abt.	755		H. Tr.				215. Inf. Div.
schw. Art. Abt. (mot)	756		H. Tr.	Stab/Art. Rgt. z.b. V. (mot)	801	II	H. Tr.
schw. Art. Abt. (mot)	757		H. Tr.	schw. Art. Abt. (mot)	801	II	H. Tr.
				Stab/Art. Rgt. z.b. V. (mot)	802		H. Tr.
schw. Art. Abt.	758		H. Tr.	Stab/Art. Rgt. z.b. V. (mot)	803		H. Tr.
schw. Art. Abt. (mot)	759		H. Tr.	Stab/Art. Rgt. z.b. V. (mot)	804		H. Tr.
schw. Art. Abt- (mot)	760		H. Tr.	schw. Art. Abt. (mot)	804	XVIII	H. Tr.
Stab/Art. Rgt. z.b. V. (mot)	760		H. Tr.	schw. Art. Abt. (mot)	808	XI	H. Tr.
schw. Art. Abt. (mot)	761		H. Tr.	schw. Art. Abt. (mot)	809		H. Tr.
							18. Art. Div.
Stab/Art. Rgt. z.b. V. (mot)	761		H. Tr.	schw. Bttr. (mot)	810		H. Tr.
Stab/Art. Rgt. z.b. V. (mot)	762		H. Tr.	schw. Bttr. (mot)	813		H. Tr.
schw. Art. Abt. (mot)	762		H. Tr.	I./Art. Rgt. (mot)	814	III	H. Tr.
schw. Art. Abt. (mot)	763	III	H. Tr.				
schw. Art. Abt. (mot)	764	V	H. Tr.	II./Art. Rgt. (mot)	814	IV	H. Tr.
Eisb. Bttr.	765		H. Tr.	schw. Art. Abt. (mot)	815	III	H. Tr.
Stab/Eisb. Art. Rgt.	766		H. Tr.	H.-Art. Stab z. b. V.	815		H. Tr.
schw. Art. Abt. z. b. V. (mot)	767		H. Tr.	schw. Art. Abt. (mot)	816	III	H. Tr.
				schw. Art. Abt. (mot)	817	IV	H. Tr.
schw. Art. Abt. z.b. V. (mot)	768	VII	H. Tr.				
schw. Art. Abt. (mot)	769	VI	H. Tr.	I./Art. Rgt. (mot)	818	XI	H. Tr.
schw. Art. Abt.	771		H. Tr.				
Stab/Art. Abt. z.b. V. (mot)	775		H. Tr.	II./Art. Rgt. (mot)	818	XI	H. Tr.
schw. Art. Abt. (mot)	777	VI	H. Tr.	III./Art. Rgt. (mot)	818	XI	H. Tr.
				H.-Art. Stab z.b. V. (mot)	818	XI	H. Tr.
H.-Art. Stab z.b. V. (mot)	779		H. Tr.	schw. Bttr. (mot)	820		H. Tr.
schw. Bttr. (mot)	779		H. Tr.	schw. Bttr. (mot)	821		H. Tr.
Stab/Eisb. Art. Rgt. z. b. V.	780	IV	H. Tr.	1. Bttr./Art. Abt. (mot)	822		H. Tr.
Stab/Eisb. Art. Rgt. z.b. V.	781		H. Tr.	schw. Bttr. (mot)	830		H. Tr.
H.-Art. Stab z.b. V.	781		H. Tr.	schw. Bttr. (mot)	833	III	H. Tr.

Troop Unit (Artillery Regt.)	Replacement District	War Structure Subordination
H.-Art.Stab z.b.V. 836 (mot)		H.Tr.
schw.Art.Abt.z.b.V.836 (mot)	II	H.Tr.
H.-Art.Stab (V) 839 (mot)		H.Tr.
schw.Art.Abt.(mot) 841	IX	H.Tr.
H.-Art.Stab z.b.V. 841 (mot)		H.Tr.
schw.Art.Abt.(mot) 842	VI	H.Tr.
schw.Art.Abt.(mot) 843	VI	H.Tr.
schw.Art.Abt.(mot) 844	IV	H.Tr.
schw.Art.Abt.(mot) 845	II	H.Tr.
schw.Art.Abt.(mot) 846	II	H.Tr.
schw.Art.Abt.(mot) 847	V	H.Tr.
schw.Art.Abt.(mot) 848	XVII	H.Tr.
schw.Art.Abt.(mot) 849	VII	H.Tr.
schw.Art.Abt.(mot) 850		H.Tr.
schw.Art.Abt.(mot) 851	VII	H.Tr.
schw.Art.Abt.(mot) 852		
schw.Art.Abt.(mot) 854	VII	H.Tr.
schw.Art.Abt.(mot) 855		H.Tr.
le.Art.Abt.(mot) 855		H.Tr.
schw.Art.Abt.(mot) 856	VI	H.Tr.
schw.Art.Abt.(mot) 857	XII	H.Tr.
schw.Art.Abt.(mot) 858	I	H.Tr.
schw.Art.Abt.(mot) 859	IX	H.Tr.
le.Art.Abt.(mot) 860	X	H.Tr.
schw.Art.Abt.(mot) 861	XX	H.Tr.
schw.Art.Abt.(mot) 862	XII	H.Tr.
schw.Art.Abt.(mot) 863	IX	H.Tr.
schw.Art.Abt.(mot) 864	IX	H.Tr.
schw.Art.Abt.(mot) 865	XIII	H.Tr.
schw.Art.Abt.(mot) 866	V	H.Tr.
Art.Rgt.(tmot) 869		3.Kav.Div.
Art.Rgt.(tmot) 870		4.Kav.Div.
schw.Art.Abt. 873		H.Tr.
schw.Art.Abt. 875		H.Tr.
schw.Art.Abt. 880		H.Tr.
schw.Art.Abt. 884		11.Pz.D.(1941)
schw.Art.Abt. 885		H.Tr.
schw.Art.Abt. 886		H.Tr.
schw.Art.Abt. 887		H.Tr.
schw.Art.Abt.(mot) 888		H.Tr.
schw.Art.Abt.(mot) 889		H.Tr.
schw.Art.Abt.(mot) 890		H.Tr.
Art.Rgt. 890	X	190.Inf.Div.
le.Art.Lehr Abt. 900 (mot)	III	Lehr-Brig.(mot) 900
schw.Art.Abt.(mot) 900	III	H.Tr.
schw.Bttr.(mot) 900	III	H.Tr.
schw.Bttr.(mot) 902		H.Tr.
schw.Art.Abt. 906		H.Tr.
schw.Bttr.(mot) 909		H.Tr.
schw.Art.Abt. 910		H.Tr.
schw.Art.Abt.(mot) 911	IV	H.Tr.
schw.Art.Abt.(mot) 912	V	H.Tr.
schw.Bttr.(mot) 922	III	H.Tr.
schw.Art.Abt.(mot) 922	III	H.Tr. / Pz.Lehr Div.
schw.Art.Abt.(tmot)923		H.Tr.

Troop Unit (Artillery Regt.)	Replacement District	War Structure Subordination
schw.Art.Abt.(tmot) 929	XII	H.Tr.
schw.Art.Abt. 930	VIII	H.Tr.
schw.Art.Abt. 931	VI	H.Tr.
Stab/Art.Rgt. 931		9.Geb.Div.
le.Art.Abt.(mot) 934		H.Tr.
le.Art.Abt.(mot) 935		H.Tr.
schw.Art.Abt.(mot) 936		H.Tr.
schw.Art.Abt.(mot) 937	V	H.Tr.
schw.Bttr.(mot) 941		H.Tr.
schw.Bttr.(mot) 943		H.Tr.
schw.Art.Abt.(mot) 956		H.Tr.
Art.Rgt.Stab z.b.V. 959 (mot)		H.Tr.
2./Art.Abt.(sf) 960		LXIV.A.K.
le.Afr.Art.Abt.(mot)961		Afr.Schtz.Rgt.961
le.Afr.Art.Abt.(mot)962		Afr.Schtz.Rgt.962
le.Afr.Art.Abt.(mot)963		Afr.Schtz.Rgt.963
le.Afr.Art.Abt.(mot)964		Afr.Schtz.Rgt.964
schw.Art.Abt.(mot) 985	V	H.Tr.
schw.Art.Abt.(mot) 986		H.Tr.
schw.Art.Abt.(mot) 987		H.Tr.
schw.Art.Abt.(mot) 988		H.Tr.
schw.Art.Abt.(mot) 989	XI	H.Tr.
schw.Art.Abt.(mot) 990		H.Tr.
schw.Art.Abt.(mot) 991		H.Tr.
schw.Art.Abt.(mot) 992	II	H.Tr.
le.Art.Abt.(mot) 993		H.Tr./LXXXV.A.K. 338.Inf.Div.
schw.Art.Abt.(mot) 997		H.Tr.
schw.Art.Abt.(mot) 998	VIII	H.Tr.
Art.Rgt.(tmot) 999		H.Tr.
Pz.Sturm Hb.Bttr. 1000-1002		H.Tr.
H.-Art.Stab z.b.V. 1020 (mot)		H.Tr.
Art.Abt. 1021	V	
Art.Abt. 1022	VI	
Art.Abt. 1023	X	
Art.Abt. 1024	XII	
Art.Abt. 1025	XII	
Art.Abt. 1026	XVII	
Art.Abt. 1027	IV	
Art.Abt. 1028	XII	
Art.Abt. 1029	VIII	
Art.Abt. 1030		
Art.Abt. 1031	VI	
Art.Abt. 1032	VI	
H.-Pak Art.Abt. 1037		H.Tr.
H.-Pak Art.Abt. 1038		H.Tr.
H.-Pak Art.Abt. 1039		H.Tr.
H.-Pak Art.Abt. 1040		H.Tr.
H.-Pak Art.Abt. 1041		H.Tr.
H.-Pak Art.Abt. 1042		H.Tr.
H.-Pak Art.Abt. 1043		H.Tr.
H.-Pak Art.Abt. 1046		H.Tr.
Art.Rgt. 1048	VIII	148.Inf.Div.
H.-Pak Art.Abt. 1052	XXI	H.Tr.
H.-Pak Art.Abt. 1053		H.Tr.
H.-Pak Art.Abt. 1054		H.Tr.

Troop Unit (Artillery Regt.)		Replacement District	War Structure Subordination
Geb. Art. Rgt.	1057	VII	157. Geb. Div.
			8. Geb. Div.
Art. Rgt.	1058	VIII	158. Res. Div.
Art. Rgt.	1059	IX	159. Inf. Div.
H. -Pak Art. Abt.	1061		H. Tr.
H. -Pak Art. Bttr.	1067		H. Tr.
Geb. Kan. Bttr.	1085		Art. Rgt. 1089
Art. Rgt.	1089	XI	189. Inf. Div.
Art. (Abt.)Rgt.	1090	X	190. Inf. Div.
Geb. Kan. Bttr.	1090		Art. Rgt. 1089
Art. Abt.	1092		H. Tr.
Bttr.	1095		H. Tr.
schw. H. -Art. Abt.	1100		H. Tr.
Art. Abt.	1131		
Art. Abt.	1132		
Art. Abt.	1133		
Art. Abt.	1134		
Art. Abt.	1135		
Art. Abt.	1136		
Art. Abt.	1137		
Art. Abt.	1138		
Art. Abt.	1139		
Art. Abt.	1140		
schw. Art. Abt.	1141		H. Tr.
schw. Art. Abt.	1143	XI	H. Tr.
schw. Art. Abt.	1145	V	H. Tr.
schw. Art. Abt.	1146	IX	H. Tr.
schw. Art. Abt.	1147	VII	H. Tr.
schw. Art. Abt.	1148	VII	H. Tr.
schw. Art. Abt.	1149	VII	H. Tr.
schw. Art. Abt.	1150	VII	H. Tr.
schw. Art. Abt.(mot)	1151	IX	H. Tr.
schw. Art. Abt.(mot)	1152		H. Tr.
schw. Art. Abt.	1154		H. Tr.
schw. Art. Abt.	1157		H. Tr.
schw. Art. Abt.	1161	V	H. Tr.
schw. Art. Abt.	1162	V	H. Tr.
schw. Art. Abt.	1163	XIII	H. Tr.
schw. Art. Abt.	1175		H. Tr.
Art. Rgt.	1176	VI	176. Inf. Div.
Art. Rgt.	1179	VIII	79. V. G. Div.
Art. Abt.	1183		H. Tr.
Art. Abt. (mot)	1194		148. Res. Div.
Eisb. Art. Abt.	1227		H. Tr.
H. -Art. Abt.	1301		H. Tr.
Art. Rgt.	1316	VIII	16. V. G. Div.
Art. Rgt.	1461	I	461. Inf. Div.
Art. Rgt.	1462	XII	462. Inf. Div.
Art. Rgt.	1541	XI	541. V. G. Div.
Art. Rgt.	1542	I	542. V. G. Div.
Art. Rgt.	1543	V	543. V. G. Div.
Art. Rgt.	1544	XVII	544. V. G. Div.
Art. Rgt.	1545		545. V. G. Div.
Art. Rgt.	1546	XVII	546. V. G. Div.
Art. Rgt.	1547	V	547. V. G. Div.
Art. Rgt.	1548	IV	548. Inf. Div.
Art. Rgt.	1549	IX	549. Inf. Div.
Art. Rgt.	1550	II	550. V. G. Div.
Art. Rgt.	1551	XX	551. V. G. Div.
Art. Rgt.	1552	V	552. V. G. Div.
Art. Rgt.	1553	V	553. V. G. Div.
Art. Rgt.	1556	XII	556. V. G. Div.
Art. Rgt.	1558	XIII	558. V. G. Div.
Art. Rgt.	1559	IX	559. V. G. Div.
Art. Rgt.	1560	X	560. V. G. Div.
Art. Rgt.	1561	I	561. V. G. Div.

Troop Unit (Artillery Regt.)		Replacement District	War Structure Subordination
Art. Rgt.	1562	I	562. V. G. Div.
Art. Rgt.	1563	III	563. V. G. Div.
Art. Rgt.	1564	XVII	564. V. G. Div.
Art. Rgt.	1565	XIII	565. V. G. Div.
Art. Rgt.	1566		566. V. G. Div.
Art. Rgt.	1567		567. V. G. Div.
Art. Rgt.	1568	IV	568. V. G. Div.
Art. Rgt.	1569	VI	569. V. G. Div.
Art. Rgt.	1571	I	571. V. G. Div.
Art. Rgt.	1572	II	572. V. G. Div.
Art. Rgt.	1599		599. Gren. Brig.
Art. Rgt.	1600		600. Gren. Div.
Art. Rgt.	1644		644. Gren. Div.
Art. Rgt.	1650		650. Gren. Div.
Art. Rgt.	1709	IX	709. Inf. Div.
Art. Rgt.	1711	XI	711. Inf. Div.
II./Art. Rgt.	1712	XII	712. Inf. Div.
Art. Rgt.	1818	X	18. V. G. Div.
Art. Rgt.	1716	VI	716. Inf. Div.

Weitere Truppenteile der Artillerie (ohne Nummer)

Troop Unit		Replacement District	War Structure Subordination
Reit. Don Kosaken Art. Abt.			1. Kos. Div.
Reit. Kuban Kosaken Art. Abt.			1. Kos. Div.
Art. Abt./Kav. Rgt. "Nord"			
Eisb. Art. Abt. z. b. V.			H. Tr.
Art. Rgt. "Afrika" 1 und 2			
Pz. Art. Abt. "Norwegen"			Pz. Div.
			Norwegen
Art. Abt. "Prag"			Div. Nr. 539
Art. Rgt. "Rhodos"			Sturm Div.
			Rhodos
Art. Rgt. "Sardinien"			Div. "Sardinien"
Art. Rgt. "Sizilien"			Div. "Sizilien"
I./Art. Rgt. "Smolensk" (bod)			Befh. H. Geb. Mitte

ARMY FLAK ARTILLERY

Troop Unit (Army Flak Art. Unit)	Replacement District	Subordination
Lehr Abt.		
GD	III	Pz.Gren.Div.GD
		Pz.Korps GD
FHH	XX	Pz.Gren.Div.
		FHH
		Pz.Korps FHH
Brandenburg	III	Pz.Gren.Div. Brdbg.
Fü.Begl.Brig.(Div.)	III	Fü.Begl.Brig.(Div.)
140		22.Pz.Div.
271	XI	13.Pz.Div.
272	XI	19.Pz.Div.
273	XVII	2.Pz.Div.
274	VI	16.Pz.Div.
275		A.O.K.17
276	IV	14.Pz.Div.
277	VIII	11.Pz.Div.
		23.Pz.Div.
278	V	23.Pz.Div.
279		A.O.K.17
280		H.Gr.Nord
		18.Art.Div.
281	VI	16.Pz.Gren.Div.
		116.Pz.Div.
282	XX	60.Inf.Div.(mot)(?)
		Pz.Gren.Div. FHH
283	I	24.Pz.Div.
284	VIII	25.Pz.Div.
		18.Pz.Gren.Div.
		24.Pz.Div.(?)
285		H.Tr.
286	III	8.Pz.Div.
287	XVII	9.Pz.Div.
288	VIII	5.Pz.Div.
289	XII	14.Pz.Div.(?)
		22.Pz.Div.
290	XIII	4.Pz.Div.
Stell.Bttr. 290		A.O.K.7
291		H.Tr.
292		H.Tr.

Troop Unit (Army Flak Art. Unit)	Replacement District	Subordination
293	V	78.Sturm Div.
294	XVII	H.Tr.
295		Pz.A.O.K.3
		20.Pz.Div.
296	IX	7.Pz.Div.
297	VII	17.Pz.Div.
298	VI	6.Pz.Div.
		2.Pz.Div.
299	IX	1.Pz.Div.
300		H.Tr.
(H.Pz.Flak Abt.) 301	III	8.Pz.Div.
302	V	10.Pz.Div.
303	II	12.Pz.Div.
(H.Pz.Flak Abt.) 304	III	26.Pz.Div.
		21.Pz.Div.(?)
305	III	21.Pz.Div.
306		H.Tr.
307		H.Tr.
308		1.Geb.Div.
309		H.Tr.
310		H.Tr.
311	XI	Pz.Lehr Div.
312	III	3.Pz.Gren.Div.
313	IX	29.Pz.Gren.Div.
314	III	3.Pz.Div.
(le.Fla.Abt.) 315	XII	15.Pz.Gren.Div.
316		H.Tr.
317		H.Tr.
318		H.Tr.
319		H.Tr.
Stell.Flak Abt. 517		A.O.K.1
Stell.FlakAbt. 518		A.O.K.1
Stell.Flak Abt. 801		A.O.K.1
Stell.Flak Abt. 802		A.O.K.1
Stell.Flak Abt. 803		A.O.K.1
Stell.Flak Abt. 804		A.O.K.1
Stell.Flak Abt. 805		A.O.K.1
Stell.Flak Abt. 806		A.O.K.7
Stell.Flak Abt. 807		A.O.K.7
999		H.Tr.
1052		H.Tr.
1255		H.Tr.
1256		H.Tr.

ARMY COAST AND FORTRESS ARTILERY

List of Troop Units

Note:

Number changes and replacement districts could hitherto be determined in only a few cases.

Troop Unit			Troop Unit		
H.K.A.Lehr Abt.; identisch mit			H.K.A.A.	10	
H.K.A.A.101 (?)			H.K.A.A.	11	
H.K.A.A.	1		Fest.A.A.	13	
H.K.A.A.	2		Fest.A.A.	16	Cherbourg
H.K.A.A.	3		H K.A.A.	19	
H.K.A.A.	5		Fest.A.A.	27	
Fest.A.R.Stb.	5		H.K.A.R.Stb.	33	
H.K.A.A.	8		H.K.A.A.	89	
H.K.A.A.	9		H.K A.Lehr Abt.	101	

Troop Unit		Replacement District	Troop Unit		Replacement District
H. K. A. R. Stb.	101		Stell. K. Bttr.	308	
H. K. Bttr.	102		Stell. K. Bttr.	309	
H. K. Bttr.	108		Stell. K Bttr.	312	
Stell. A. A.	118		Stell. K. Bttr.	313	XIII
			Stell. K. Bttr.	314	
H. K. Bttr.	121		Stell. K. Bttr.	315	
H. K. Bttr.	126		Stell. K. Bttr.	316	
Stell. K. Bttr.	127		Stell. K. Bttr.	317	
Stell. K Bttr.	130		Stell. K. Bttr.	318	
Stell. K. Bttr.	133		Stell. K. Bttr.	324	
Stell. K. Bttr.	135		H. K. A. R. Stb.	325	
Stell. K. Bttr.	136		H. K. A. A.	338	
H. K. A. A.	141		Stell. K. Bttr.	344	
H. K. A. A.	142	XII	Stell. K. Bttr.	345	
H. K. A. A.	143	VII	Stell. K. Bttr.	348	
H. K. A. A.	144	VI	Stell. K. Bttr.	350	
H. K. A. A.	145		Stell. K. Bttr.	351	
H. K. A. A.	147		H. K. Bttr.	353	VI
H. K. A. A.	148	VI	H. K. Bttr.	354	VI
H. K. A. A.	149	XI	H. K. Bttr.	355	VI
H. K. Bttr.	154		H. K. A. R. Stb.	356	
Stell. K. Bttr.	159		H. K. Bttr.	356	VI
Stell. K Bttr.	164		H. K. Bttr.	361	III
Stell. K. Bttr.	165		H. K. Bttr.	362	XII
Stell. K. Bttr.	166		H. K. Bttr.	363	XIII
Stell. K Bttr.	167		H. K. Bttr.	364	XIII
H. K. A. R. Stb.	180		K. Bttr.	3. / 367	
(H. K. A. R. Dänemark)					
			H. K. Bttr.	374	
Fest. A. R. Stb.	200	XXI	H. K. Bttr.	375	
H. K. A. R. Stb.	207	II	H. K. A. A.	401	VI
Stell. Bttr.	212		K. Bttr.	3. / 402	
H. K. Bttr.	212		H. K. Bttr.	402	
Stell. A. A. Stb.	215		H. K. A. A.	404	
			H. K. Bttr.	405	
Stell. A. A. Stb.	216				
			Stell. K. Bttr.	409	
Stell. Bttr.	217		Stell. K. Bttr.	411	
			Stell. K. Bttr.	413	
Stell. Bttr.	220		Stell. K. Bttr.	414	
			Stell. K. Bttr.	415	
Stell. Bttr.	222		H. K. Bttr.	416	
Stell. Bttr.	224				
Stell. Bttr.	227		Stell. K. Bttr.	417	
Stell. Bttr.	230		Stell. K. Bttr.	419	
H. K. A. A.	231		Stell. K. Bttr.	420	
Stell. Bttr.	232		Stell. K. Bttr.	421	
Stell. Bttr.	237		H. K. Bttr.	431	
Stell. K. Bttr.	237		H. K. Bttr.	432	
Stell. Bttr.	242		H. K. Bttr.	433	
Stell. Bttr.	247		H. K. Bttr.	434	
Stell. Bttr. .	252		H. K. A. R. Stb.	437	XVII
Stell. K. Bttr.	252		H. K A. R. Stb.	438	
H. K. Bttr.	253		H K. A. A. Stb.	438	
Stell. Bttr.	257		H. K. A. R. Stb. z. b. V.	439	
Stell. Bttr.	262		H. K. A. A. Stb.	439	
Stell. K. Bttr.	264		H. K. A. A.	440	
Stell. K. Bttr.	265		H. K. A. A.	441	
Stell. K. Bttr.	266		H. K. A. A.	442	
Stell. Bttr.	272				
H. K. Bttr.	272		H K. A. A.	443	
H. K. Bttr.	274		H K. A. A.	444	
H. K. A. A. Stb.	274		H. K. A. A.	447	
H. K. Bttr.	275		H. K. A A.	448	
Stell. Bttr.	282		H. K. A. A. Stb.	452	
H. K. Bttr.	282		H. K. A. A.	453	
H. K. A. A.	283		H. K. Bttr.	454	
H. K. A. A.	284		H. K. Bttr.	455	
H. K. A. A.	285				
H. K. A. A.	287	VII	H. K. A. A.	455	
H. K. A. A.	288	VIII	H. K. A. A.	457	
H. K. A. A.	289		H. K. Bttr.	461	

Troop Unit		Replacement District	Troop Unit		Replacement District
H.K.Bttr.	462		K.Bttr.	2./520	
H.K.Bttr.	463		H.K.A.A.	520	
H.K.Bttr.	464		H.K.A.A.	521	
H.K.Bttr.	465		H.K.Bttr.	522	
H.K.Bttr.	466		H.K.A.A.	523	III
H.K.Bttr.	467		H.K.Bttr.	524	
H.K.Bttr.	468	III	H.K.Bttr.	525	
H.K.Bttr.	469		H.K.A.R.Stb.	527	
H.K.Bttr.	470		H.K.A.A.Stb.	527	
H.K.Bttr.	471		H.K.A.A.	528	XIII
H.K.Bttr.	472		H.K.A.A.	529	IX
H.K.A.A.	473		H.K.A.A.	531	III
H.K.A.A.	474	X	H.K.A.A.	533	XII
H.K.A.A.	475		H.K.A.A.Stb.	534	
H.K.A.R.Stb.	476		H.K.Bttr.	534	
K.Bttr.	1./477	XVIII	H.K.A.A.	535	
			H.K.Bttr.	537	
K.Bttr.	2./477	XVIII	H.K.Bttr.	538	
H.K.A.A.	477	XVIII	H.K.A.A.	540	
H.K.A.A.	478	V	H.K.Bttr.	541	
H.K.A.A.	479	VI	H.K.Bttr.	542	
H.K.A.A.	480	XIII	H.K.Bttr.	543	
			H.K.Bttr.	545	
H.K.A.A.	481		H.K.Bttr.	546	
			H.K.Bttr.	547	
H.K.A.A.	482				
H.K.A.A.	483		H.K.Bttr.	548	
H.K.A.A.	484	VI	H.K.Bttr.	549	
H.K.A.A.Stb.	485	VI	H.K.Bttr.	550	
H.K.A.A.Stb.	486	VI	H.K.Bttr.	552	
H.K.A.A.Stb.	487		H.K.A.R.Stb.	553	
H.K.A.A.Stb.	488		Stell.K.Bttr.	554	
H.K.A.A.Stb.	489		Stell.K.Bttr.	555	
H.K.A.A.Stb.	490		Stell.K.Bttr.	556	
H.K.A.A.Stb.	491		H.K.Bttr.	558	
H.K.A.A.Stb.	492		H.K.Bttr.	561	
H.K.A.A.Stb.	493	III	H.K.Bttr.	562	
H.K.A.A.Stb.	494		H.K.Bttr.	563	
H.K.A.A.Stb.	495		H.K.A.A.Stb.	563	
H.K.A.A.Stb.	496		H.K.Bttr.	564	
H.K.A.A.Stb.	497				
H.K.A.A.(Stb.)	498		H.K.Bttr.	567	
			H.K.Bttr.	569	
H.K.A.A.	499		H.K.Bttr.	570	
H.K.A.A.	500		H.K.Bttr.	571	
H.K.Bttr.	502		H.K.Bttr.	572	
H.K.A.A.Stb.	502		H.K.Bttr.	573	
H.K.Bttr.	503		H.K.Bttr.	574	
H.K.A.A.Stb.	503		H.K.Bttr.	575	
H.K.A.A.Stb.	504		H.K.Bttr.	576	
H.K.A.A.Stb.	505	VI	H.K.Bttr.	577	
H.K.Bttr.	506		H.K.Bttr.	578	
H.K.Bttr.	507		H.K.Bttr.	579	
H.K.Bttr.	508		H.K.Bttr.	580	
H.K.A.R.Stb.	509		H.K.Bttr.	581	
Stell.A.A.Stb.	510	XIII	H.K.Bttr.	584	X
			H.K.Bttr.	585	
			H.K.Bttr.	588	
			H.K.Bttr.	589	
H.K.A.A.	510	XIII	H.K.Bttr.	590	
H.K.Bttr.	511		H.K.Bttr.	591	
H.K.Bttr.	512		H.K.Bttr.	592	
H.K.Bttr.	513		H.K.Bttr.	593	
H.K.Bttr.	514		H.K.Bttr.	596	
H.K.Bttr.	515		H.K.Bttr.	598	
H.K.Bttr.	516		H.K.Bttr.	599	
H.K.Bttr.	519		H.K.Bttr.	601	
K.Bttr.	1./520		H.K.A.R.Stb.	610	
			H.K.Bttr.	611	

Troop Unit		Replacement District
H.K.Bttr.	612	
H.K.Bttr.	613	
H.K.Bttr.	616	
H.K.Bttr.	622	
H.K.Bttr.	628	
H.K.Bttr.	630	
H.K.Bttr.	644	
H.K.Bttr.	645	
H.K.A.R.Stb.	649	
H.K.A.R.Stb.	656	
H.K.Bttr.	667	
H.K.Bttr.	673	
H.K.A.R.Stb.	677	
H.K.A.A.	677	
H.K.Bttr.	678	
H.K.A.R.Stb.	680	
H.K.A.R Stb.	697	V
H.K.A.R.Stb.	699	
H.K.A.A.	702	
K.Bttr.	1./706	
K.Bttr.	2./706	
H.K.A.A.Stab	706	
H.K.A.A.	707	
H.K.A.A.	708	
H.K.A.A.	709	
Stell.Bttr.	715	
H.K.A.A.	716	
Stell.Bttr.	719	
H.K.A.R.Stb.	720	
H.K.A.A.	722	
Stell.Bttr.	724	
H.K.A.A.	724	
H.K.A.A.	728	V
H.K.A.A.Stb.	728	
K.Bttr.	1./729	
K.Bttr.	1.-3./730	
Stell.Bttr.	734	
Stell.A.A.Stb.	738	
Stell.Bttr.	739	
H.K.Bttr.	739	
H.K.Bttr.	742	
H.K.Bttr.	744	
H.K.Bttr.	745	VI
H.K.Bttr.	746	VI
H.K..Bttr.	747	
H.K.Bttr.	748	
H.K.A.A.Stb.	750	
H.K.Bttr.	751	
H.K.A.R.Stb.	752	II
H.K.A.A.Stb.	754	
H.K.A.A.(Stb.)	755	
H.K A.A.(Stb.)	756	
H.K.A.A.Stb.	757	
H.K.A.R.Stb.	758	
H.K.A.A.Stb.	758	
H.K.A.A.Stb.	759	
H.K.A.A.	766	
Stell.A.A.Stb.	769	VI

Troop Unit		Replacement District
Stell.Bttr.	1.-3./769	VI
H.K.A.A.Stb.	769	VI
Stell.A.A.	770	XI
H.K.A.A.	770	XI
Stell.Bttr.	771	
H.K.A.A.	772	XII
H.K.A.A.	773	
H.K.Bttr.	774	
H.K.A.A.	778	
Stell.Bttr.	784	
Stell.K Bttr.	784	
Stell.A.A.	789	IV
H.K.A.A.	789	IV
H.K.A.R.Stb.	791	
Stell.A.A.	799	
H.K.A.A.	799	
Stell.Küst.Bttr.	799	
H.K.A.A.	803	
H.K.A.A.Stb.	805	VIII
Stell.K.Bttr.	806	
Stell.K.Bttr.	807	
H.K.A.A.	808	IX
H.K.A.A.	809	XI
H.K.A.A.Stb.	812	
H.K.Bttr.	813	VI
H.K.A.A.Stb.	819	
H.K.A.A.	820	
H K.A.A.	821	
H.K.A.A.	822	
H.K.A.A.(Stb.)	823	
H.K.A.R.Stb.	824	
H.K.A.R.Stb.	825	
H.K.A.A.(Stb.)	826	VI
H.K.A.A.(Stb.)	827	VII
H.K.A.A.(Stb.)	828	
H.K.A.R.Stb.	828	
H.K.A.A.(Stb.)	829	VII
H.K.A.A.(Stb.)	831	VII
H.K.A.A.	832	IX
H.K.A.A.	833	III
H.K.A.A.	834	XII
H.K.A.A.	835	
H.K.A.R.Stb.	836	VI
H.K.A.R.Stb.	837	VII
H.K.A.A.	838	
H.K.A.R.	839	
H.K.A.R.Stb.z.b.V.	840	
H.K.A.A.	841	
H.K.Bttr.	843	
H.K.A.A.	850	XII
H.K.A.A.	852	
H.K.A.R.	853	
H.K.Bttr.	862	
H.K.Bttr.	863	
H.K.Bttr.	864	
H.K.Bttr.	865	
H.K.Bttr.	866	

Troop Unit		Replacement District	Troop Unit		Replacement District
H.K.Bttr.	869		H.K.A.A.Stb.	947	
H.K.Bttr.	870		H.K.Bttr.	948	
H.K.A.R.Stb.	876		H.K.A.A.Stb.	948	
H.K.Bttr.	877		H.K.Bttr.	949	
H.K.Bttr.	880		H.K.A.A.Stb.	949	
H.K.Bttr.	883	XVIII	H.K.Bttr.	950	
H K.Bttr.	884		H.K.A.R.Stb.	950	
H.K.Bttr.	885		H.K.Bttr.	951	
			H.K.Bttr.	952	
H.K.Bttr.	887		H.K.Bttr.	953	
H.K Bttr.	888		H.K.Bttr.	954	
H.K.Bttr.	889		H.K.A.A.Stb.	955	
H.K.Bttr.	890		H.K.Bttr.	956	
H.K.Bttr.	892		H.K.A.R.Stb.	956	
H.K.A.A.Stb.	893		H.K.Bttr.	957	
H.K.Bttr.	894	XI	H.K.A.A.(Stb.)	957	XIII
H.K.Bttr.	895		H K.Bttr.	958	
H.K.Bttr.	896		H.K.Bttr.	959	
H.K.Bttr.	897		H.K.Bttr.	960	
H.K.Bttr.	898		H.K.Bttr.	961	
H.K.Bttr.	899		H.K.Bttr.	962	
H.K.A.A.Stb.	901	V	H.K.Bttr.	963	
H K.A.A.Stb.	903	III	H.K.Bttr.	964	
Stell.Bttr.	904		H.K.Bttr.	966	
			H K.Bttr.	967	
Stell.Bttr.	905		H.K.A.A.Stb.	967	
Stell.K.Bttr.	905		H.K.Bttr.	970	
H.K.A.A.	906	VI	H.K.A.R.Stb.	970	
H.K.Bttr.	907		H.K.Bttr.	971	
			H.K.A.R.Stb.	971	
H.K.A.A.	910	X	H.K.Bttr.	972	
H.K.A.A.	911	IV	H.K.A.R.(Stb.)	972	
H.K.A.R.Stb.	912				
Stell.Bttr.	913				
H.K.A.A.Stb.	914		H.K.Bttr.	973	
Stell.Bttr.	915		H.K.A.R.Stb.	973	
H.K.A.R.Stb.	917		H.K.Bttr.	974	
H.K.A.R.Stb.	919		H.K.A.R.Stb.	974	
H.K.A.R.(Stb.)	920	X	H.K.Bttr.	975	
			H.K.A.R.Stb.	975	
			H.K.Bttr.	976	
			H.K.A.R.Stb.	976	
			H.K.Bttr.	977	
			H.K.A.R.(Stb.)	977	
			H.K.Bttr.	978	
			H.K.A.R.Stb.	978	
H.K.Bttr.	921		H.K.Bttr.	979	
H.K.A.R.Stb.	922		H.K.A.R.(Stb.)	979	
H.K.A.R.Stb.	927				
H.K.Bttr.	927				
H.K.A.A.	928	V	H.K.Bttr.	980	
H.K.A.A.	929	XII	H.K.A.R.Stb.	980	
H.K.Bttr.	930		H.K.Bttr.	981	
			H.K.A.R.(Stb.)	981	VI
H.K.A.R.Stb.	931				
H K.Bttr.	931		H.K.Bttr.	982	
			H.K.A.R.Stb.	983	
H.K.Bttr.	932		H.K.Bttr.	983	
H.K.A.R.Stb.	932		H.K.Bttr.	984	
H.K.Bttr.	933		H.K.Bttr.	985	
H.K.A.A.(Stb.)	933		H.K.Bttr.	986	
H.K.Bttr.	937		H.K.Bttr.	987	
H.K.A.R.Stb.	938		H.K.Bttr.	988	
H.K.A.R. Stb.	940		H K.Bttr.	989	
H.K.Bttr.	941		H.K.Bttr.	990	
H.K.Bttr.	942		H.K.Bttr.	991	
H.K.Bttr.	943		H.K.Bttr.	992	
H.K.Bttr.	944		H.K.Bttr.	993	
H.K.Bttr.	945		H.K.A.R.Stb.	993	
H.K.A.R.Stb.	945		H.K.A.R.Stb.	994	
H.K.Bttr.	946		H.K.Bttr.	995	
H.K.A.A.Stb.	946				
H.K.Bttr.	947				

Troop Unit		Replacement District		Troop Unit		Replacement District
H.K.A.Bttr.	996			H.K.A.R.Stb.	1240	VI
H.K.A.R.Stb.	997			H.K.A.A.	1242	
H.K.Bttr.	997			H.K.A.A.	1243	
H.K.Bttr.	998			H.K.A.A.	1244	VII
H.K.Bttr.(Abt.)	999			H.K.A.R.Stb.	1245	VI
H.K.A.R.Stb.	1000			H.K.A.R.Stb.	1246	
H.K.A.A.Stb.	1001			H.K.A.R.Stb.	1247	
H.K.A.R.Stb.	1006			H.K.A.R.Stb.	1248	
Fest.Bttr.	1073			H.K.A.A.	1251	
Fest.Bttr.	1074			H.K.A.R.Stb.	1252	X
Fest.A.A.	1078			H.K.A.R.Stb.	1253	XII
H.K.A.R.Stb.	1101			H.K.A.R.Stb.	1254	XII
H.K.A.R.Stb.	1102	IX		H.K.A.A.	1254	
H.K.A.R.Stb.	1103			H.K.A.A.	1255	
H.K.A.A.	1104			H.K.A.A.	1260	
H.K.A.A.	1105			H.K.A.R.Stb.	1261	II
H.K.A.R.Stb.	1105			H.K.A.A.	1261	
H.K.A.A.	1106			H.K.A.R.Stb.	1262	VII
H.K.A.A.	1107			H.K.A.R.Stb.	1265	III
H.K.A.A.	1108	XIII		H.K.A.R.Stb.	1266	II
H.K.A.A.	1109			H.K.Bttr.	1271	II
H.K.A.A.	1110			H.K.Bttr.	1272	II
H.K.A.A.	1111			H.K.Bttr.	1273	II
H.K.A.A.	1112	IX		H.K.Bttr.	1274	II
H.K.A.A.	1113			H.K.A.R.Stb.	1280	IV
H.K.A.A.	1114			H.K.A.A.	1282	
H.K.A.A.	1115	IV		H.K.A.R.Stb.	1287	II
H.K.A.A.	1116	IV		H.K.A.R.Stb.	1290	X
H.K.A.A.	1117				1291	X
H.K.A.A.	1118			H.K.A.R.Stb.	1294	
H.K.Bttr.(Abt.)	1119			H.K.A.R.Stb.	1296	
Fest.A.A.	1121			H.K.A.R.Stb.	1298	
Fest.A.A.	1127			Fest.A.A.	1301	
Fest.A.A.	1132			Fest.A.R.Stb.	1303	XII
Fest.A.A.(Rgt.)	1133			Fest.A.A.	1303	XII
				Fest.A.A.	1305	
Fest.A.A.	1134			Fest.A.A.	1306	
H.K.A.A.	1147			Fest.A.A.	1308	
H.K.A.A.	1148			Fest.A.A.	1309	
H.K.A.A.	1149			Fest.A.A.	1310	
H.K.A.A.	1150			Fest.A.A.	1311	
Art.Abt.(bod.)	1180	IV		Fest.A.A.	1313	
Art.Abt.(bod.)	1181	XVII		Fest.A.A.(Rgt.)	1314	
Art.Abt.(bod.)	1182			Fest.A.A.	1315	I
Art.Abt.(bod.)	1189			Fest.A.R Stb.	1321	
H.K.A.A.	1190	III		Fest.A.A.	1505	
H.A.A.(bod.)	1190	III		Fest.A.A.	1506	
H.K.A.A.	1191	X		Fest.A.A.	1509	
schw.Art.Abt.(bod.)	1191	X		Fest.A.A.	1510	
H.K.A.A.	1192	VI		Fest.A.A.	1514	
schw.Art.Abt.(bod.)	1192	VI		Fest.A.A.(Rgt.)	1515	V
H.K.A.A.	1193			le.Fest.A.A.	1516	III
schw.Art.Abt.(bod.)	1193	VIII		Fest.A.A.	1517	XII
H.K.A.A.	1194			Fest.A.A.	1518	XII
schw.Art.Abt.(bod.)	1194	III		Fest.A.A.	1519	XII
H.K.A.A.	1195	IX		Fest.A.A.	1520	XII
Art.Abt.(bod.)	1195	IX		Fest.A.A.	1521	XII
H.K.A.A.	1196			Fest.A.A.	1522	XII
Art.Abt.(bod.)	1196			Fest.A.A.	1523	XII
H.K.A.A.	1197	IV		Fest.A.A.	1524	XII
Art.Abt.(bod.)	1197	IV		Fest.A.A.	1525	XII
H.K.A.A.	1198	XII		Fest.A.A.	1526	XII
schw.Art.Abt.(bod.)	1198	XII		Fest.A.A.	1527	XII
				Fest.A.A.	1532	XII
schw.Art.Abt.(bod.)	1199			Fest.A.A.	1535	
H.K.A.R.Stb.	1202			Fest.A.A.	1539	
H.K.A.R.Stb.	1218			Fest.Art.Abt.I./	1716	
H.K.A.R.Stb.	1224			Fest.A.R.Frankfurt/Oder		III
H.K.A.R.Stb.	1226			Fest.A.R.Königsberg		I
H.K.A.A.	1230			H.K.A.R.Littoria		
H.K.A.A.	1231			Fest.Art.Grp.Belfort		

RECONNAISSANCE ARTILLERY

Note:

1. Until October 1939, the observation units (B.-Abt.) belonged to the division troops (Div. 1st Wave), or in a few cases to the corps troops.

With few exceptions, these units were motorized.

After the Polish campaign, all observation units were moved to the army troops. Their structure remained unchanged for the time being, consisting of

Staff, intelligence platoon, printing troop, weather troop (as of the end of 1941, united in one staff battery).
1st (measuring) battery, 2nd (sound-measuring) battery, 3rd (light-measuring) battery.

In the instructional unit and units 1, 4, 5 and 6, the 4th (balloon) battery (with three light machine guns and two 2 cm anti-aircraft guns), already existing in peacetime, remained for the time being.

2. In each of the Panzer divisions, an armored observation battery (light platoon, heavy platoon, measuring platoon, printing troop) was established in 1940-1941. In 1942-1943 they were they were moved to the Panzer artillery regiments.

3. In 1942 the observation units were changed into light observation units as follows:

a. The measuring batteries and measuring troops were removed from the observation troops, and light and heavy measuring batteries were established within the measuring and map troops; measurement evaluation platoons were established in the sound- and light-measuring batteries.

b. The existing balloon batteries were divided, as balloon platoons and balloon troops (plus hydrogen generation troops, either motorized or ground) into individual light observation units.

The light observation units now consisted of staff with staff battery, 1st (sound-measuring) battery, 2nd (light-measuring) battery and, in part, balloon platoon or troop. The position observation units or observation units (ground) set up after August 1942 were similarly structured.

4. For the army artillery (Volks-Artillerie) corps, special fire control batteries and observation batteries were established as of the end of 1943.

5. The following special formations of the observation troops can be named:

a. weather platoons (mot) and (o)
b. mobile weather platoons (ground)
c. observation instructional units and instructional batteries for weather platoons (as of 1/1/43)(see section on artillery instructional units)
d. mountain observation batteries
e. light sound-measuring batteries (mot) (LL)
f. experimental weather platoon "Würzburg" (radar)(1943)
g. magnetic measuring battery (1) (1942, a platoon at first)
h. light velocity-measuring troops (mot)
i. heavy velocity-measuring troops (mot)
j. astronomical measuring platoon (also troop)

On this subject, the sound-measuring troops of the infantry (see infantry section) and the measuring and targeting platoons of the heavy artillery may also be mentioned.

Troop Unit		Replacement District		Troop Unit		Replacement District
B.-Abt. (mot)	1	I		B.-Abt. (mot)	33	XII
				B.-Abt. (mot)	34	XII
B.-Abt. (mot)	2	II		B.-Abt. (mot)	35	V
B.-Abt. (mot)	3	III		B.-Abt. (mot)	36	XII
				B.-Abt. (mot)	37	
B.-Abt. (mot)	4	IV		Geb. B.-Abt. (mot)	38	XVIII
(sp. als le. Abt. b.				B.-Abt. (mot)	40-43	
18. Art. Div.)				B.-Abt. (mot)(bod)	44	
B.-Abt. (mot)	5	V				
B.-Abt. (mot)	6	VI		Stell. B.-Abt.	49	
B.-Abt. (mot)	7	VII		Stell. B.-Abt.	52	
B.-Abt. (mot)	8	VIII		ab 1940; zeitw. auch (bod)		
B.-Abt. (mot)	9	IX		Stell. B.-Abt.	54	
B.-Abt. (mot)	10	XIII		Stell. B.-Abt.	56	
B.-Abt. (mot)	11	I		Stell. B.-Abt.	57	
B.-Abt. (mot)	12	II		1940 aufgest.; zeitw. (bod)		
B.-Abt. (mot)	13	XI		B.-Abt. (bod)	58-61	
B.-Abt. (mot)	14	IV		B.-Abt. (bod)	59	XI
B.-Abt. (mot)	15	IX		B.-Abt. (bod)	63-64	
B.-Abt. (mot)	16	VI		Stell. B.-Abt.	65	
B.-Abt. (mot)	17	XIII				
B.-Abt. (mot)	18	VIII		B.Abt. (tmot)	71	
le. Geb. B.-Abt.	18	XVIII		B.-Abt. (tmot)	72	
B.-Abt. (mot)	19	XI		Pz. Beob. Bttr.	88	
B.-Abt. (mot)	20	X		le. Beob. Bttr.	92	
B.-Abt. (mot)	21	I		Ballon Bttr.	100-101	
B.-Abt. (mot)	22	X				XI
B.-Abt. (mot)	23	III				
B.-Abt. (mot)	24	IV		Pz. Beob. Bttr.	320	XVII
B.-Abt. (mot)	25	V		Pz. Beob. Bttr.	321	XVII
B.-Abt. (mot)	26	VI		Pz. Beob. Bttr.	322	V
B.-Abt. (mot)	27	VII		Pz. Beob. Bttr.	323	XI
B.-Abt. (mot)	28	VIII		Pz. Beob. Bttr.	324	XIII
B.-Abt. (mot)	29	IX		Pz. Beob. Bttr.	325	IX
				Pz. Beob. Bttr.	326	XII
B.-Abt. (mot)	30	X		Pz. Beob. Bttr.	327	III
B.-Abt. (mot)	31	XI		Pz. Beob. Bttr.	328	III
B.-Abt. (mot)	32	II		Pz. Beob. Bttr.	329	II

Troop Unit		Replacement District	Subordination [the longer notes in the listing]
Pz. Beob. Bttr.	330	IX	1. Pz. Div.
Pz. Beob. Bttr.	331	VI	6. Pz. Div.
Pz. Beob. Bttr.	332	IV	14. Pz. Div.
Pz. Beob. Bttr.	333		
Pz. Beob. Bttr.	334	VIII	11. Pz. Div.
Pz. Beob. Bttr.	335	IX	20. Pz. Div.
Pz. Beob. Bttr.	336	IV	18. Pz. Div.
sp. Nr. 88 (18. Art. Div.)			
Pz. Beob. Bttr.	339		
Beob. Bttr.	388	II	V. Art. K. 388
auch Feuerleitbttr. 388			
Beob. Bttr.	401	XIII	V.-Art. K. 401
Es bestanden daneben teilw. auch Feuerleitbttr. in der Nr.-Gruppe 401-411			
Beob. Bttr.	402	IX	V.-Art. K. 402
Beob. Bttr.	403	XI	V.-Art. K. 403
Beob. Bttr.	404	X	V.-Art. K. 404
Beob. Bttr.	504	II	V.-Art. K. 405
Beob. Bttr.	406	III	V.-Art. K. 406
Beob. Bttr.	407	V	V.-Art. K. 407
Beob. Bttr.	408	XVII	V.-Art. K. 408

Beob. Bttr.	409	VII	V.-Art. K. 409
Beob. Bttr.	410	XIII	V.-Art. K. 410
Beob. Bttr.	411		H.-Art. K. 411
B.-Abt. (bod)	554	V	554. Stell. Div. 1939/40; H. Tr. 1940/
B.-Abt. (bod)	555	XI	555. Stell. Div. 1939/40; 41
			1940/41 H. Tr.
B.-Abt. (bod)	556	XX	556. Stell. Div. 1939/40;
			1940/41 H. Tr.
B.-Abt. (bod)	557	IV	557. Stell. Div. 1939/40;
			1940/41 H. Tr.
Astron. Meßzug	700		
Beob. Bttr.	776	II	V.-Art. K. 776
Beob. Bttr.	1095		V.-Art. K. 1095
B.-Abt. "Afrika" (mot)		I/III	Afrikakorps/Pz. Gr. Afrika
Astron. Meßtrupp	1		ebenso
"Afrika"			

-In Addition-

light velocity-measuring troops (mot)	501, 502, 504, 506, 507, 509, 511, 512, 514, 516, 518, 519, 521, 526
velocity troops (mot)	601 (I. /Art. Rgt. 84), 602 (Stb. Eisb. Art. Rgt. 702), 603 (Art. Abt. 703 ?), 604 (Eisb. Bttr. 710), 605 (I. /Art. Rgt. 84), 606 (Eisb. Bttr. 686), 607 (Eisb. Bttr. 712), 613 (Eisb. Bttr. 689), 614 (I. /Art. Rgt. 84), 615 (Eisb. Bttr. 722), 616 (Art. Abt. 800), 617 (Eisb. Bttr. 713)
weather platoons (mot)	502-512,
mobile weather platoons (mot)	502, 535, 711
magnetic measuring batteries (mot)	653 (originally magnet-measuring platoon, later battery with 26 troops)

MEASURING AND MAP TROOPS
MILITARY-GEOGRAPHICAL SERVICE OFFICES

Note:

In addition to the map offices of the divisions and corps (generally numbered the same as the division and corps troops), a series of measuring units (mot) (Verm. Abt.) were established among the army troops and those of the armies in East Prussia (A.O.K.) when the war broke out.

By including parts of the observation artillery, there resulted, in the summer and autumn of 1941, a new type of artillery troops in the form of measuring and map troops.

As of November 15, 1939, the Measuring Instructional and Replacement Unit was established, later to be included in the Artillery Instructional Regiment.

List of Troop Units and Service Offices:

Chief of the War Map and Measurement Services (Kr K Verm Chef)
        established" November 1, 1941, in the Army General Staff

War Map Command (as of 1944)
Highest officer of the War Map and Measurement Services East (Warsaw) (as of April 1, 1942), Southeast (Prague)
        (as of April 1, 1942), Northeast, West
Work Staff for War Map Measurement Services, Athens
German Military Cartographic Institutes in Minsk, Prague and Warsaw (became War Map Measurement Offices)

War Map Measurement Offices 1-10 (as of June 1, 1942) (Warsaw, Riga with branches in Dorpat, Kovno,
        Reval), Minsk, Kiev, Kharkov, Prague, Belgrade, Utrecht, Paris, etc.
Map Office z.b.V. (Foreign Armies West)
Measuring Unit z.b.V. (Verm. Staff. z.b.V.)
Geographical Groups: Paris (mobile), with branch in Marseilles (mobile),
        Radom (mobile), Athens (mobile) with branch in Saloniki, Belgrade, Brussels,
        Bucharest, Hilversum, Copenhagen, Krakow, Riga, Rovno

The measuring and map troops were essentially organized as follows as of 1942-1943:

Army Groups:

Each with one (light) Measuring and Map Unit (mot) (also Panzer and tropical) with staff, one measuring battery (mot), one map battery (mot) (one photo and printing platoon, one mapmaking platoon, one transport platoon) or one light map-printing unit (mot); in 1944-1945, what had hitherto been army group map offices (no.-group 600) were united with these units.

Army High Command:

Similar or immediately in number group 500; in 1944-1945, addition of the army map offices (A.Kart.St.) (formerly army map stores).

General Command:

Each with one corps map office (mot) (previously corps map store); by the war's end there were also border map stores.

Division Command:
Division map office (mot) or in a few cases also (ground).

The field position of a leFH 16 battery on the Atlantic coast before the 1944 invasion; as in 1914-18, camouflage nets have been removed in "alarm" situation – pointless against the enemy superiority from air and sea.